Somaliland's Private Sector at a Crossroads

A WORLD BANK STUDY

Somaliland's Private Sector at a Crossroads

*Political Economy and Policy Choices
for Prosperity and Job Creation*

WORLD BANK GROUP

Contents

Tables

Acknowledgments

This report was jointly produced by a team from the World Bank Group led by Peter Mousley and Jade Ndiaye from the Trade and Competitiveness Global Practice in the Africa Region, together with Joshua Wimpey and Mohammad Amin from the Enterprise Survey team in the World Bank's Development Economics Group; Cari Votava and Marco Nicoli from the Finance and Markets Global Practice; Christian Eigen-Zucchi from the Development Economics Prospects Group and specialist consultants Kenneth Menkhaus and David Phillips.

In addition to the editors listed above, Carlo Corazza and Alana Fook from the Finance and Markets Global Practice, and Abdi Rashid Hassan, a land specialist from Somaliland, also contributed to this report through the technical papers that were prepared as background analysis. The team would also like to acknowledge the advice and contributions of Michael Engman and Thilasoni Benjamin Musuku from the Trade and Competitiveness and Finance and Markets Global Practices, respectively; Najeeb Hashi, the World Bank SomPREP II Regional Coordinator in Somaliland; and Austin Mwape, the World Bank advisor to the Bank of Somaliland.

Written comments on earlier drafts were received from the following colleagues: Najy Benhassine, Guillemette Jaffrin, Stephen Ndegwa, Samuel Maimbo, Gary Fine, and Adhan Haji.

While the content of this report is entirely the responsibility of the World Bank team that prepared it, the team would like to express its deep thanks in particular to His Excellency Saad Shire, former Minister of National Planning and Development, and His Excellency Mohamed Omar, former Minister of Commerce and Investment, Government of Somaliland, for their sustained engagement and guidance on this study. Also, the team would like to extend its sincere thanks to the many other Government of Somaliland and private sector counterparts, who contributed their input and participation during the meetings and the workshops undertaken as part of the consultation process that accompanied the preparation of the report.

Executive Summary

Report Objectives, Data, Structure, Themes, and Process

Objectives: This report is the World Bank's first effort to undertake an in-depth, consultative, evidence-based analysis of private and financial sector development in Somaliland* in at least a generation. The objective of the report is to take stock of what has been achieved to date since Somaliland passed its 1999 Constitution, provide an assessment of the current evolution of the private sector, and identify priority policy options and related actions that would best enable the private sector to generate the growth and jobs sought under the 2012-16 Somaliland National Development Plan (SNDP).

Data: This report was made possible through the funds put in place by multiple donors[1] under the Somalia Private Sector Development Re-Engagement Program Phase II (SomPREP II), the support and commitment to the exercise on behalf of the Government of Somaliland (GoS), and the ready participation of a wide range of Somaliland private and financial sector stakeholders and diaspora spokespersons. The report is based on a series of technical notes[2] prepared over a period from June 2013 to April 2014, based on data gathered through both a formal and informal enterprise survey from January through April 2013, a *Doing Business* Report on Hargeisa presented in Somaliland in October 2012, data gathered from Somaliland Business Fund (SBF) project proposals, a wide-ranging dialogue process with diaspora across four continents, comprising focus groups in some 10 cities, and independent interviews conducted by project team staff.

Structure and Themes: The report is structured around three key sector "actors" of the economy: enterprises, financial institutions, and the government. This approach was taken to facilitate a "political economy" lens into the analysis. In all societies, legislation and policy formulation are debated and adopted in a context of sometimes cooperative and sometimes countervailing efforts by

---

*The focus in this report is on Somaliland based on the World Bank's experience of working on private sector development issues there since 2007. Today, the World Bank program is operational across Somalia, including in Puntland and parts of southern and central regions, working also in areas such as public finance management, governance and infrastructure. Although Somaliland claimed independence from Somalia in 1991, it is not a member country of the World Bank. For more information on the Bank's work please visit: http://www.worldbank.org/en/country/somalia

social, economic, and political actors to protect and advance their interests. This political arena can be crowded with private sector, civic, and political party stakeholders engaged in a combination of competition, bargaining, influence buying, and collusion, all in pursuit of public policy outcomes that serve their particular needs. Those needs may or may not coincide with the national interest. Interest group-driven politics are an essential part of a vibrant polity, notwithstanding that they can produce what economists, development planners, and many citizens would consider suboptimal outcomes. Such outcomes can manifest in the form of resistance to needed reforms, delays, unwieldy compromise legislation, or laws and policies that reflect the influence of powerful interest groups. Hard choices are a challenge for all types of political systems, but new democracies and those featuring low levels of institutionalization confront special challenges when facing difficult decisions for the sake of long-term development. This is especially the case when policy reforms require short-term sacrifices or risk taking by vocal social groups or powerful economic actors.

This report employs a political economy lens to explore trends in, opportunities for, and impediments to effective government regulation of the private sector and private sector-led economic growth in Somaliland, a relatively new democracy with weak institutions. The report looks at the interplay of power, interests, and relationships of key political, economic, and social actors in government and the private sector. It also seeks to take into consideration the sociocultural context in which the people of Somaliland are striving to enhance their livelihoods and ensure their security, and how that social setting shapes public policy and private sector decision making. The methodology employed specifically for this political economy dimension is qualitative. It consists of semi-structured interviews in Somaliland and abroad with a sample of civil servants, elected officials, businesspeople, civil society figures, diaspora members, local and foreign analysts, officials from donor agencies, and foreign investors. The analysis also draws extensively on the surveys, other technical papers, and data referenced earlier, as well as existing secondary literature on Somalia.

The 2011 *Conflict, Security and Development* and 2013 *Jobs* World Development Reports (WDR)[3] provided further guidance in the preparation of the report. In the case of the 2011 report, the emphasis placed on institutional legitimacy and the sensitivity required in following through on a calibrated reform agenda that provides justice and jobs and manages the political interests at stake was at the core of the analysis undertaken for this report. As the 2011 report states, regulatory simplification and private sector job creation are potentially major components of an effective strategy to transform institutions while fostering societal legitimacy (World Bank 2011, 17). The support of the private sector for a reform strategy centered on its role as job creator is fundamental to its success. And there is no other sustainable alternative. As the 2013 WDR states, "*…the private sector is the main engine of growth of job creation and the source of roughly nine out of ten jobs in the world…*" (World Bank 2013, 58). And, as will be seen, while there is a critical need to develop Somaliland's civil service—including the recruitment of quality expertise and the strengthening of regulations and procedures—fiscal and other constraints will not permit the public sector to serve as a significant source of new employment over the future.

Process: It is also intended that the ongoing research and analysis undertaken for this report be used to stimulate policy and wider stakeholder debate to further inform its recommendations. To this end, the World Bank team undertook two separate rounds of consultations with government clients and key private sector counterparts in June and November 2013 and then an open workshop organized in partnership with the GoS that took place in Hargeisa on March 20, 2014. This full-day event brought the World Bank team in dialogue through plenary consultations and breakout sessions with over 100 representatives of government, municipal, private, financial, nongovernmental organizations (NGOs), and donor sectors. It was a huge testament to the active and committed interest of Somalilanders in the continuing development of their economy. Their input was crucial to the analysis, key findings, and recommendations contained in this final report.

Key Findings

Context

Somaliland has already experienced two decades of major changes in its security situation, its political system, its economy, the regional environment, and technological changes.[4] In the process, Somaliland and its people have demonstrated impressive resilience and adaptability. The Somaliland of today bears very little resemblance to the Somaliland emerging from the war and dislocations of the early 1990s. Politically, Somaliland featured very significant innovation in the 1990s, from the Boroma peace conference to the passage of the Constitution in 1999, which transitioned the government from a clan-based form of representation to a multiparty system. Somaliland also demonstrated its political adeptness with the hybrid governance model it developed, which enshrined the role of customary authorities (clan elders) in the Upper House or Guurti. In a region with various forms of more authoritarian government, Somaliland remained committed to a liberal democratic model.

Despite the years of destruction brought on by the civil war, Somaliland has been the site of impressive levels of economic recovery due to: (a) the ability of the government and society to maintain peace and security; (b) a durable social contract ensuring a sufficient degree of inclusivity and negotiation in matters of politics, disputes, and allocation of resources and employment across clan lines; (c) high flows of remittances from the large Somaliland diaspora; (d) a robust private sector which has emerged since 1991; and (e) a powerful cultural tradition of honoring mutual obligations within extended lineage groups, which facilitates greater social trust, the flow of finances in the form of informal loans or gifts, and mutual indebtedness. The Somaliland economy is driven by the private sector. Unlike most other economies in the world, the government footprint is limited, amounting to under 10 percent of the gross domestic product (GDP). This context is both a structural advantage and constraint to its further growth and the capacity of the private sector to create the number of jobs demanded by a growing population, after a generation of hard work building a political system and economy from the remains of a destructive civil war. The report strives to take stock of the progress to date in private sector performance and development and to identify policy priorities that the government, in partnership with the private sector, can pursue in furtherance of job creation and growth objectives.

The resilience, vibrancy, and innovation of Somaliland's private sector are there to be seen for all. With a very limited enabling environment and minimal government support, it has succeeded in delivering a range of key goods and services to the population. The private sector role in telecommunications, remittances, livestock and trade, and other service sectors—including the delivery of health and education services—makes for a unique type of public–private partnership. But the limitations are mounting. The enterprise survey comparing results to other comparator economies shows Somaliland to have some of the most extreme constraints to access to finance, land, and transport. The tax regime is also a tightly binding constraint. In the face of these challenges, government capacity to deliver key regulatory and promotional services related to access to land and transport services appear to be undermined by a lack of policy focus in part due to political and other considerations, related resource constraints, and an inability to measure performance against policy objectives. This is especially evident with respect to the development of the financial sector, which is at present stalled.

Over the past 15 years, the political system can be seen struggling to respond to changes in the economy, society, and wider regional setting, and it is having difficulty keeping up with changes in the private sector. Everywhere, political institutions and governance models tend to be slower to adapt than their counterparts in civil society and the private sector, so Somaliland is not unique on this score. Politics is driven and constrained by competing interests, compromises, and oft-times slow decision-making processes. In the case of contemporary Somaliland, the gap between the speed of potentially transformational changes in the wider political economy and the slow pace of formal government policy response runs the risk of missed opportunities on a large scale. This includes the capacity to capture these opportunities—if they arrive—for the greater public interest. At the heart of this challenge is the issue of economic governance.

Sector Review

Each chapter of the report, as summarized below, provides diagnostic findings and policy recommendations pertaining to the three key economic agents that are the report focus—namely, the enterprise, financial, and government sectors.

Somaliland Private Sector: Principal characteristics of this private sector are summarized in box ES.1.

Box ES.1 The Somaliland Private Sector

1. As of 2012, *Somaliland's GDP is estimated to be US$1.390 billion* (excluding official development assistance). The largest sector is livestock, comprising a 29.5 percent share of GDP, followed by wholesale and retail trade (19.5 percent), crops (8.2 percent), real estate activities (6.4 percent), forestry (5.2 percent), construction (3.7 percent), and information and communication (2.2 percent).

2. The private sector is largely informal and only a small percentage of companies are formally registered with the Ministry of Commerce and Investment. *The most comprehensive data on firms in Somaliland come from the Municipal license lists, which show a total number of 14,100 licenses issued in 2012, mostly in trade, construction, and business services.*

3. Based on the *Doing Business in Hargeisa* 2012 report, *Hargeisa ranks 174 out of 183 economies on the ease of doing business.* Hargeisa's low rankings can largely be explained by an incomplete legal and regulatory framework, overly burdensome administrative procedures, high costs and low compliance with regulation.

4. The *cultural and societal factors that make the Somaliland private sector unique* include high levels of trust (among people living in the same neighborhood, in the same establishment, in the same company, and in the same local community) as well as relatively low levels of crime.

Based on data from the enterprise survey in Somaliland, the median sales growth rate in Somaliland is 10 percent per annum and the mean value is 13.8 percent. Growth in sales is highly correlated with variables such as the structure of the firm, level of competition, gender composition of the owners, and the level of trust and security as perceived by firms. Some key correlates with sales growth include the following:

- Growth in sales is higher among firms that report facing a larger number of competitors.
- Faster-growing firms have a worse perception of law enforcement than slower-growing firms.
- The median growth rate in payrolls is 16 percent (per annum), and the mean growth rate is 29 percent. The growth rate in payrolls is significantly higher for relatively young firms.
- Access to finance is the most commonly cited obstacle to business in Somaliland (selected by 49 percent of firms), followed by access to land (selected by 25 percent of firms). Other obstacles include transportation, tax rates, and electricity.

Some entry points for new employment generation pertain to both innovation and women-headed and/or primarily female-owned businesses. These are summarized in box ES.2.

Box ES.2 Enhancing Enterprise Performance—Policy Options for the Short and Medium Term

1. *Support innovating firms in the service sector,* which have higher productivity and sales performance with less exposure to larger infrastructure constraints. They offer a higher probability in the short term to create new jobs and market opportunities.
2. *Support women-owned businesses,* which are the primary driver of female employment in the economy. Evidence in Somaliland strongly suggests that firms with women in top positions tend to have a higher proportion of female workers than other firms and potential to upgrade productivity over the short term, a *prima facie* reason to focus support to this segment of the enterprise sector.
3. Other shorter-term options for employment creation include *Support to the formalization of businesses and the promotion of start-ups in Somaliland* through acceleration of the establishment of a one-stop shop for business registration, registration streamlining, and augmentation of promotional services (including enterprise support services, technical and vocational training, and other business services).
4. *Key priorities over the longer term for the enterprise sector* include development of a Berbera corridor; development and implementation of a Land Use Master Plan; implementation of the 2012 Doing Business in Hargeisa recommendations, particularly the introduction of a modern company law and investment law; and improved government implementation of regulatory services.

Financial Inclusion and Product Diversification: The financial sector in Somaliland lacks the fundamental legal, policy, and regulatory building blocks to enable greater financial inclusion and intermediation. These factors are indicative of a financial sector still in its infancy, which is largely informal and unregulated. Some other key features of the sector are as follows:

• Remittances inflows to over 40 percent of households are a major economic lifeline to Somaliland, one of the most remittance-dependent economies in the world. Remittances estimates for Somaliland range from US$500–900 million per year, equivalent to 35–70 percent of GDP.
• The Bank of Somaliland (BoS) has established neither a National Payment System (NPS) infrastructure nor adequate laws and regulations to govern financial intermediary activities and ensure compliance with international *Anti-Money Laundering* (AML) and *Combatting the Financing of Terrorism* (CFT) requirements.
• Remittances companies in Somaliland currently offer a limited range of financial products, including savings and current accounts, trade finance, letters of credit, and mobile payment services, as well as Islamic financing products (principally, "*murabaha*" and "*musharaka*").

Attempts to broaden the availability of effectively regulated financial products and services have been constrained by the legal and regulatory framework,

---

**Box ES.3 Strengthening Financial Sector Inclusiveness and Diversification—
Policy Options for the Short and Medium Term**

1. On a priority basis, initiate and implement *legal and policy actions* including: (a) a broad-based informed public policy consultation involving recognized Sharia jurists to clarify important provisions in the Islamic Banking Law and the pros and cons of commercial banking; (b) passage of the AML-CFT bill to prevent criminal abuse of the financial system and bolster remittance channels; (c) implementation of licensing and registration systems, including screening processes that identify all beneficial owners, assessment of internal governance systems, and effective "fit and proper" screening of all applicant entities; and (d) establishment of internal integrity systems and professional standards for BoS to become a credible supervisory and regulatory authority of the financial sector.

2. Establish a *time-bound "Roadmap of Actions"* required to put in place the necessary laws, regulations, systems, and procedures identified to be currently lacking; assign accountable officials responsible for roadmap implementation; and establish an associated capacity building strategy and program to support the BoS to undertake all supervisory and regulatory functions needed.

3. Adopt a *legal framework and National Payment System* so that principles of security, accountability and inclusiveness can be achieved.

4. In the medium to longer term, extend *support services (for example, technical assistance, matching grants) to licensed financial institutions* to assist these entities to develop and mitigate risks of certain types of financing, including noncollateral-based lending and equity and investment instruments that can extend financial access to businesses.

---

including delays to the passage of the draft conventional banking bill highlighted as a policy priority in the SNDP. Key priorities for the financial sector are summarized in box ES.3.

Government Sector: The GoS plays a crucial role in delivering services to the private sector, specifically in its role to (a) regulate and (b) promote private sector development (PSD) activities and identify key areas for institutional change and capacity building as economic recovery and development proceeds. The government has a small revenue base (estimated at US$80–100 million, or approximately 5 percent of GDP), and weaknesses in the civil service persist, including—among other challenges—a shortage of qualified staff, informality of decision making, *ad hoc* changes in the structure of ministries, and overlaps between government ministries in relation to scope of responsibilities. Based on a survey administered to 11 government ministries in which a self-assessment tool was used to rank overall capacity in key regulatory and promotional areas, the average ranking for all responding agencies was just below the midpoint score of 5.0 (in a range from 0 to 10) for regulation and a significantly lower score of 3.6 for promotion. The problems for government are largely tied to internal capacity problems (shortage of funds, equipment/facilities, shortage of

---

Box ES.4 Strengthening Government PSD Regulatory and Promotional Capacity

1. *Critical choices need to be made regarding the further development of regulatory and promotional functions of government services to the private sector.* This will need to take into account the generally higher level of expertise and fiscal implications of promotional activities.
2. Given the current level of capacity and expertise, *the development of promotional functions should be designed around a clear private sector development strategy.*
3. *Constraints are evident on both the regulatory and promotional sides of government services to the private sector.*
4. *Key shorter term priorities for the public sector include capacity building especially in supervision, enforcement and monitoring and inspection.* Capacity building support should be closely linked to policy reform and implementation performance with a focus in the short term on the ministries and entities responsible for more binding constraints to private sector development, together with institutional commitment to implement.
5. *The future balance of central and local government action merits review.* A large part of the responsibility could beneficially focus at the local government level, although in the short-term local capacity does not yet exist.

---

skilled staff, and so on) and problems connected with the external environment (incompleteness of laws/regulations, disputes between outside parties, lack of credibility of government decisions). The implications are summarized in box ES.4.

The Political Economy Dimension

Somaliland's political economy today is replete with both high risks and significant opportunity, which puts a premium on getting economic governance policies right and remaining proactive and vigilant about emerging trends. First, the **current risks**:

- **Missed opportunities.** Somaliland's economic growth and development have the opportunity for a significant boost if policies and laws supportive of the enterprise and financial sectors are implemented. On the horizon are potentially oil and increasing seaport revenues. Inertia—resistance to adaptation and reform—and failure to develop the institutional capacities to effectively deploy and utilize these resources (including over the immediate term through priority enterprise and financial sector reform actions) could potentially squander this opportunity.

- **Lack of government autonomy.** Every liberal democracy faces a delicate balance between protecting political space for interest articulation by the public (usually via interest groups) and protecting government autonomy from powerful groups attempting to "capture" public policy for parochial gain. At present, Somaliland's government is vulnerable to capture by private sector interests, which constrains its ability to take policy actions for the public good. As pressure mounts for passage of key legislation to promote good economic governance, interest groups with a stake in the status quo will work to block reform.

- **Instability and destabilization.** Somaliland has shielded itself from the instability that has plagued much of the Horn of Africa but remains vulnerable, especially to terrorist attacks by al-Shabaab. Instability generated by political or clan tensions is less likely but cannot be ruled out, especially if public unhappiness over poor government performance and limited economic opportunities rises.

- **External shocks.** Somaliland is highly vulnerable to external shocks. These will remain a risk over which Somaliland has little control for the foreseeable future. Policies by governments or private firms that restrict or interrupt the flow of remittances are the current chief danger. Economic downturns or restrictions in immigration policies that affect the outflow of Somaliland migrant laborers or their ability to earn money abroad are another. Changes in trade policies by countries like Saudi Arabia have in the past had magnified consequences on Somaliland and, in the future, if trade increases with Ethiopia, its trade policies will have that potential as well.

- **Jobless growth.** One of the biggest political dangers facing Somaliland is jobless growth. This tension will grow if progress is not made now before a potential extractive industry boom, which all too often will intensify expectations in what is generally a sector associated with high revenues but limited direct job potential. Sharp increases in wealth amidst high unemployment is a recipe for instability. Good stewardship of current opportunities—in particular establishing a robust enabling environment for wider PSD—and the downstream growth and effective utilization of government revenues from these new industries will be critical to the realization of socially acceptable job growth.

The future opportunities are as follows:

- **New sources of revenues.** The possibility of windfall profits from any combination of the new economies that could emerge in Somaliland—oil, other extractive industries, expanded trade with Ethiopia, sectors making use of the fiber-optic cable—constitute a historic, unprecedented opportunity for transformational growth and development.

- **Market position.** Somaliland's geographic position plays to its favor in multiple directions. Berbera is well-placed to serve shipping though the Red Sea and enjoys excellent access to the booming economies of South Asia, the affluent economies of the Gulf states, and the emerging economy of Ethiopia.

- **Direct foreign investment (DFI).** Global investment capital has increasingly looked to Africa—or parts of Africa—as the most promising site for high returns on investment. While Somaliland remains high risk, the recent flow of DFI is promising and could constitute the beginning of more outside investment in the economy.

- **Diaspora.** Somaliland enjoys an exceptional advantage with its large, committed, and increasingly well-established diaspora. Its mature diaspora has acquired new skill sets and capital abroad and is ready to harness both if conditions appear favorable.

- **Public opinion.** Somaliland possesses an invaluable asset in its vibrant democracy and open society, where civil society can be mobilized and political leaders must be mindful of the public's views. The government should ensure that this civil society is fully informed of the unprecedented new economic opportunities that could present themselves in Somaliland. The public are an essential partner if the government are to be able to implement the reforms that will ensure these opportunities serve the wider public interest.

Choices for the Future

The economy is at a crossroad. It requires a step-change towards more formal economic governance arrangements in some of its key sectors. These are objectives that the GoS has itself highlighted for action in its *National Development Plan 2012–16*. While sovereignty issues do impede the government from taking prompt action in some arenas, there is wide scope for it to proceed to address policy priorities that will position the economy to take on the challenges it will face over the period of the *Somaliland National Vision 2030*. These include the following areas, which, if accomplished, would have significant positive ramifications for economic growth and job creation:

- **Financial Sector:** First and foremost and over the short term, Somaliland needs to get its financial sector into better shape. This is the lifeblood of the economy. The government should pursue and conclude decisively on its current ongoing debate as to the nature of this sector and whether it is to be a solely Islamic financial system or alternatively a dual system. Once this decision is made, the government should move purposefully to amend and introduce the necessary legislation so that an effective regulatory system can be operationalized and this absolutely key sector can provide the inclusive services that the economy so desperately needs.

- **Enterprise Sector:** In the short term, facilitate formalization and new business entry and target services to those businesses with near-term employment and growth potential, including firms with a track record for innovation and female-headed businesses. Over the longer term, develop enterprise zones and industrial parks where it will be possible to mitigate infrastructure and land access risks more systematically. Ensure that these services are allocated to interested businesses in a transparent and accountable manner and in accordance with well-defined and well-documented eligibility criteria. The other key infrastructure investment priority over the medium to longer term must be the development of the Berbera Corridor. This is not just about capital investment. It must also entail governance development and modernization of other key related services—in particular, the customs administration.

- **Government Sector:** Ensure that capacity building and investment in government and other public agencies (for example, the BoS and Berbera Port) is aligned closely to policy milestones and the passage of critical legislative instruments and regulations and initiatives being taken for the enterprise and finance sector—as outlined above. Put in place a metrics program and align institution building and training closely to progress on these higher-level development outcomes.

Notes

1. This includes Department for International Development, United Kingdom (DFID), Danish International Development Agency (DANIDA), and the World Bank State and Peace Building Fund (SPF).

2. This includes technical notes on the formal and informal enterprise sectors, the diaspora, the remittance sector, government institutions, access to land, and political economy.

3. World Bank (2011, 2013).

4. Somaliland—while a self-declared independent state—has not been formally recognized by the international community, and as such remains for legal purposes a subsovereign territory within Somalia. Nevertheless, the term Somaliland is used throughout this report.

Abbreviations

AG	Attorney General
AML/CFT	anti-money laundering/combatting the financing of terrorism
BoS	Bank of Somaliland
CDD	customer due diligence
CPIA	Country Public Institutional Assessment
CSC	Civil Service Commission
CSI	Civil Service Institute
CSR MC	Civil Service Reform Ministerial Steering Committee
DAI	Development Associates International
DANIDA	Danish International Development Agency
DFI	direct foreign investment
DFID	Department for International Development, United Kingdom
EEZ	Exclusive Economic Zone
ES	enterprise survey
FCS	fragile and conflict-affected states
FSNAU	Food Security and Nutrition Analysis Unit
FAO	Food and Agriculture Organization (of the UN)
GBP	Great Britain Pounds
GDP	gross domestic product
GDS	Global Development Solutions
GoS	Government of Somaliland
HBB	household-based business
IFC	International Finance Corporation
IGR	Institution and Governance Review
ILO	International Labour Organization
MFRs	Ministerial Functional Reviews
MoCI	Ministry of Commerce and Investment
MoF	Ministry of Finance
MoPWHT	Ministry of Public Works, Housing and Transport

MSW	Municipal Solid Waste
MTOs	money transfer operators
NGO	Nongovernmental Organization
NPS	National Payment System
ODA	official development assistance
OECD	Organisation for Economic Co-operation and Development
OSS	one-stop shop
PER	Public Expenditure Review
PPP	public–private partnership
PSD	private sector development
RPW	remittance prices worldwide
RSP	remittance service provider
SBF	Somaliland Business Fund
SME	small and medium-sized enterprise
SNDP	Somaliland National Development Plan
SomPREP II	Somalia Private Sector Development Re-engagement Program Phase II
SOMSA	Somali Money Services Association
SPF	World Bank State and Peace Building Fund
SSA	Sub-Saharan Africa
TEU	Twenty-Foot Equivalent (container)
UAE	United Arab Emirates
UNDP	United Nations Development Program
UN	United Nations
US$	United States Dollar
USAID	United States Agency for International Development
VAT	Value Added Tax
WDR	World Development Report

CHAPTER 1

Introduction

Objectives

The Somaliland economy is driven by the private sector. Unlike most other economies in the world, the government footprint is limited, amounting to under 10 percent of the gross domestic product (GDP). As will be presented in this report, this context is both a structural advantage and constraint to further economic growth and the capacity of the private sector to create the jobs demanded by a growing population, after a generation of hard work building a political system and economy from the remains of a destructive civil war. The report strives to take stock of the progress to date in private sector performance and development and to identify policy priorities that the government, in partnership with the private sector, can pursue in furtherance of job creation and growth objectives. The target audience for this report is principally the Government of Somaliland (GoS) and its private and financial sectors. The report also hopes to contribute to the work of Somaliland's other development partners.

To this end, the report commences with an overview of the structure of the private sector and a recap of the business environment within which it operates, drawing for this latter aspect on the findings of the *Doing Business in Hargeisa 2012* report (World Bank and IFC 2012). The report then proceeds with a more in-depth look at the characteristics of the three key "sectors" that drive the Somaliland economy— the private, financial, and government sectors—and the factors that impact their overall performance in achieving government policy objectives, as set out in the GoS's document titled Somaliland National Vision 2030. The specific issues addressed include, as requested by the GoS, enterprise formalization, financial inclusion, government capacity, and economic governance. This is most appropriate, as the analysis clearly points to these issues being of primary importance to the achievement of a growing and job-creating economy. The report concludes with some recommended short-, medium-, and longer-term policy priorities for each of the three key sectors.

Methodology

The report draws on a range of analytical inputs, complemented by interviews, workshops, and lessons learned from the work done under the multidonor-funded Somaliland Private Sector Development Re-engagement Program Phase II (SomPREP II).[1] A summary of the analytical instruments and technical studies that went into the preparation of this report are summarized below.

- **Enterprise Surveys:** The World Bank team conducted a survey of formal and informal private businesses in Somaliland. These surveys are designed to capture the structure, conduct, and performance of private firms in Somaliland, as well as the quality of the business climate, broadly defined to include various elements such as the availability of physical infrastructure, the law and order situation, access to finance, labor regulations and issues regarding obtaining licenses and permits. Where possible, a comparison is made between Somaliland and comparator countries, which include Afghanistan, Ethiopia, Rwanda, Timor-Leste, and Yemen. Only key findings germane to the principal themes arising out of the consultation process and as agreed with the GoS are considered in this report. The Enterprise Survey (ES) was conducted from October 2012 to March 2013 and was based on 500 private sector[2] enterprises in seven of the largest cities in Somaliland (Hargeisa, Lasanood, Wajaale, Berbera, Burao Borama, and Erigavo). The survey included micro enterprises with less than five employees, as well as larger firms, formal manufacturing firms, gums and resins, telecoms, remittance companies, retail, construction, hotel, and other enterprises. The establishments were identified from registrations with the Ministry of Commerce and Investment (MoCI), the Attorney General's office, and local municipalities, thus giving a representative picture of the formal private sector. A second survey of 443 informal household-based businesses (HBBs) was also conducted to capture the informal private sector experience. In addition to data on firm productivity, two types of information on the investment climate were collected: (a) subjective or perception measures of what managers see as the major obstacles faced by their firms; and (b) objective indicators such as production lost due to power outages and amount of time managers spend dealing with government regulations.

- **Access to Land Technical Note:** This is based on research in Hargeisa, Burao, and Borama that entailed interviews and document research, as well as a case study approach to some land dispute cases to better elucidate the problems faced by the private sector.

- **The Diaspora Technical Note:** This is based on analysis of transcriptions of focus group interviews, supported by data from the *Doing Business in Hargeisa* study and the Somaliland Enterprise Survey. The focus group interviews were conducted in 2013 with diaspora participants in Hargeisa and eight Somaliland diaspora hubs—Cardiff, Birmingham, London,

Dubai, Toronto, Ottawa, Columbus, and Minneapolis. Small informal interviews were also held in Djibouti and Nairobi. The events were intended to attract large numbers of diaspora business investors, some of whom were preidentified for interviews and others of whom volunteered to participate leading up to or following the launch event. A total of 68 interviewees participated in the discussions, with an average of eight interviewees per session. The discussions varied in average length from 45 minutes to an hour. The participants were asked questions from a questionnaire that sought to determine: (a) how long participants had been investing in Somaliland and in what sectors; (b) the key determinants for the selection of sectors and opportunities; (c) the biggest obstacles or constraints to investment; (d) factors influencing investment decision making (for example, levels of trust, relations with family members and previous success). The approach sought to capture detail from individual investors on investment decisions within an economic, political, and social context.

- **The Remittance Sector Technical Note:** This is based on the January 2007 General Principles for International Remittance Services (General Principles).[3] The General Principles provide best practices and guidelines for efficient remittance markets and have been endorsed by various international organizations, including the Financial Stability Forum and the G8 and G20 group of countries. Among other things, the technical note recommends assessments of national remittance market compliance with the recommendations of the General Principles. Recommendations are also made as to possible actions to be taken to improve their application for Somaliland.

- **The Government Institutions Technical Note:** This differs from the standard approaches to analyzing public institutional structure and performance, such as: (a) Ministerial Functional Reviews (MFRs); (b) Institution and Governance Reviews (IGRs); (c) Country Public Institutional Assessments (CPIAs); and (d) Public Expenditure Reviews (PERs), some of which have been undertaken in Somaliland (by the United Nations [UN] and World Bank, for example). Instead, this study looks at government institutions through the lens of their engagement with private business. The coverage of the survey concerns: (a) regulatory functions; and (b) promotional activities. A scoring system was used to assess the level of private business engagement of each agency. The agencies with maximum engagement were then mapped against the key constraints facing private business to determine the critical actions required to alleviate the constraints.

- **The Political Economy Note:** This applies both political economy and political anthropology lenses to assess key economic governance issues in Somaliland. The note identifies emerging structural changes and dynamics in the Somaliland economy, as well as political developments that could pose new challenges or opportunities. The main political economy risks and opportunities facing Somaliland in the next three to five years are also highlighted. Consideration is also given to economic governance issues from a conflict prevention perspective, drawing on recent World Bank research on resilience and vulnerability to conflict (World Bank 2011). The methodology employed for this political economy dimension is qualitative. It is based on the body of previous academic and other work and a series of semi-structured interviews conducted during three missions over a period from June 2013 to March 2014. These interviews—in both Somaliland and abroad—involved a sample of civil servants, elected officials, business people, civil society members, local and foreign analysts, officials from donor agencies, and foreign investors. The analysis also draws on the surveys, other technical papers, and data that has been prepared for this report, as well as existing secondary literature on Somalia.

Structure and Themes of Report

This report is structured around three key sector "actors" of the economy, that is, enterprises, financial institutions, and the government. This approach was taken to facilitate a "political economy" lens into the analysis. In all societies, legislation and policy formulation are debated and adopted in a context of sometimes cooperative and sometimes countervailing efforts by social, economic, and political actors to protect and advance their interests. This political arena can be crowded with private sector, civic, and political party stakeholders engaged in a combination of competition, bargaining, influence buying, and collusion, all in pursuit of public policy outcomes that serve their particular needs. Those needs may or may not coincide with the national interest. Interest group-driven politics are an essential part of a vibrant polity, notwithstanding that they can produce what economists, development planners, and many citizens would consider suboptimal outcomes, in the form of resistance to needed reforms, delays, unwieldy compromise legislation, or laws and policies that reflect the influence of powerful interest groups. Hard choices are a challenge for all types of political systems, but new democracies and those featuring low levels of institutionalization confront special challenges when facing difficult decisions for the sake of long-term development. This is especially the case when policy reforms require shorter-term sacrifices or risk taking by vocal social groups or powerful economic actors.

The report explores from a political economy perspective trends in, opportunities for, and impediments to effective government regulation of the private sector and private sector-led economic growth in Somaliland, a relatively new democracy with weak institutions. Its primary focus is on the interplay of power, interests, and relationships of key political, economic, and social actors in government and the private sector. It also accounts for the sociocultural context in which the people of Somaliland seek to enhance their livelihoods and ensure their security and how that social setting shapes public policy and private sector decision making.

The 2011 *Conflict, Security and Development* and 2013 *Jobs* World Development Reports (WDR; World Bank 2011, 2013) provided further guidance in the preparation of the report. In the case of the 2011 WDR, the emphasis placed on institutional legitimacy and the sensitivity required in following through on a calibrated reforms agenda that provide justice and jobs and manages the political interests at stake was at the core of the analysis undertaken for this report. As the 2011 report states, regulatory simplification and private sector job creation are potentially major components of an effective strategy to transform institutions while fostering societal legitimacy (World Bank 2011, p. 17). The support of the private sector centered on its role as job creator is fundamental to the success of a reform strategy. As the 2013 WDR states, "...*the private sector is the main engine of growth of job creation and the source of roughly nine out of ten jobs in the world*"(World Bank 2013, 58). While there is a critical need to develop Somaliland's civil service—including the recruitment of quality expertise and the strengthening of regulations and procedures—fiscal and other constraints will not permit the public sector to serve as a significant source of new employment in the future.

Stakeholder Consultations

The report was prepared based not just on the above analysis framework but also in close cooperation with the GoS and other stakeholders. This comprised a formal series of consultations commencing in June 2013, when the first round of enterprise survey data was available and when the World Bank team met with the key government departments and some leading business interests. A subsequent round of consultations was held, including focus group sessions with the Chamber of Commerce, when the informal enterprise data became available and the results of the diaspora dialogues became available.

After further work required to complete the Remittance Sector, Access to Land, and Political Economy technical notes, a one-day workshop comprising over 100 participants was held in Hargeisa to discuss the analytical findings with a focus on certain themes as requested by the GoS. These themes are reflected in the main chapters of this report—addressing issues of enterprise development and formalization, financial inclusion, government capacity, and economic governance.

Notes

1. This is a World Bank-executed US$24.6 million Multi-Donor Trust Fund supported by Department for International Development, United Kingdom (DFID), Danish International Development Agency (DANIDA), and the World Bank State and Peace

Building Fund (SBF). An additional US$4.9 million has been mobilized for a tugboat project initiated out of preparatory work financed under the SomPREP II project.

2. Detailed information on the Enterprise Surveys methodology and data are available on the website www.enterprisesurveys.org.

3. Bank for International Settlements and the World Bank (2007).

CHAPTER 2

Background to the Somaliland Private Sector

The Setting

Somaliland's private sector has thrived in many ways since Somalilanders charted a path out of the destruction inflicted on the region during the Siad Barre regime. The extent of its revival since 1991 is a testament to the Somaliland people and their entrepreneurial and business culture. The private sector, part of a broad set of businesses anchored in the agropastoral, telecommunications, trading, and financial/remittance sectors but also in provision of social services, has rightly been acknowledged for its resilience and contribution to an economy and people that experienced massive dislocation and privation prior to the fall of the Siad Barre regime in 1991. By then, the capital city of Hargeisa had largely been reduced to rubble, with an estimated 70 percent of the city destroyed, some 5,000 people killed, and 500,000 people internally displaced.

Since this time and in parallel with an extraordinary effort of Somalilanders to rebuild the region and establish a legitimate and viable government institutional structure, the private sector has shown a level of innovation, vibrancy, and capacity for investment risk that has been rightly lauded as fundamental to the success story that is Somaliland. The World Bank (2006) Somalia Country Economic Memorandum referred to this private sector in the following terms:

> *In all regions, the private sector is providing sometimes better and more efficient services than the state before the civil war, as in telecommunications*—an international phone call costs 50 cents per minute, the cheapest rate anywhere in Africa—*and air transport*—Daallo Airlines flies Paris-Djibouti for 40 percent of the price of Air France. *Sometimes it is doing so less reliably and efficiently, as in electricity, water, and sanitation*—but service is now available in towns that never benefited from those services in the previous autocratic regime. *And sometimes, as in the case of banking services and roads, only minimal services are available.* The private sector also offers *essential social services*, including health and education, whose coverage in some cases extends beyond peak levels achieved under the previous regime. Even in the areas of *court services*—dispute resolution, contract enforcement, property rights protection, and law and order—Somalis have largely relied on private solutions based on traditional clan customs.

Despite the variety of obstacles—including the legacy of underdevelopment and war, large-scale population displacement, a modest resource base, and lack of diplomatic recognition—Somaliland has been the site of impressive levels of economic recovery and activity since 1991. These gains have been based mainly on five factors: (a) the ability of the government and society to maintain peace and security; (b) a durable social contract ensuring a sufficient degree of inclusivity and negotiation in matters of politics, disputes, and allocation of resources and employment across clan lines; (c) high flows of remittances from the diaspora, which underwrite much of Somaliland's consumer economy; (d) a robust private sector, which has emerged since 1991; and (e) a powerful cultural tradition of honoring mutual obligations within extended lineage groups, which facilitates greater social trust, the flow of finances in the form of informal loans or gifts, and mutual indebtedness. This latter feature gives Somaliland households and businesses a high level of "social capital" on which to draw and is a valuable source of economic stability in an otherwise high-risk investment environment.

The means by which Somaliland's economic growth has been achieved have involved pragmatic tools—negotiations, informal governance arrangements, reliance on pluralistic legal systems, and deals struck between political authorities and private sector figures. Much of what constitutes economic governance in Somaliland since 1991 comprises oral agreements rather than formal contracts and application of law. This degree of informality in economic governance reflects both a long-standing feature of Somali political culture—the binding nature of customary law and a strong preference for negotiated oral agreements—and a practical response to the reality that Somaliland's fledgling government in the past lacked the capacity to play a robust enabling and regulatory role for the private sector.[1]

In 2011, the GoS published the Somaliland long-term vision statement titled *Somaliland: The Way Forward 2030 and SNDP 2012-16.* It proposed a development program based on the five pillars of (a) economic development; (b) infrastructure development; (c) governance and the rule of law; (d) social development; and (e) environmental protection. These documents highlight many of the issues to be addressed in this report. They talk of the need to support the private sector to generate jobs and the imperative of the government to reduce the cost of doing business and to foster firm start-up and growth through financial and infrastructure development that will leverage private investment. They also talk of the need for more robust legislative and regulatory frameworks.

Progress towards these goals, now in the final two years of the SNDP five-year period, has been limited, and, with elections planned in 2017 there is limited time available for the current administration to lock in targeted SNDP policy outcomes before a new political mandate is established that may well take Somaliland in different directions. Some of these current policy priorities constitute what could rightly be seen as "game changers" for the future evolution of Somaliland's private sector. To add urgency to the call for action, the report also touches upon transformational economic events that could take place during the period of the *2030 Vision*. If experience internationally provides any guidance, these events could change the focus of policy for many generations to come. At stake is a development agenda that seeks to promote a diversified, efficient, employment-oriented private sector-led economy that serves the broad base of the population. Given the opportunities and risks, the window of opportunity for this agenda is relatively short term and may not reappear with the same favorable enabling conditions. This is not a window to be foregone lightly. This report discusses further these potential "game changing" initiatives and the associated opportunities and costs by taking into account the political economy dynamics at play in Somaliland's policy decision-making process.

The Size and Structure of the Somaliland Private Sector

GDP Shares: The continuing significance of the private sector to the Somaliland economy is most immediately evident when viewed in terms of GDP shares. Reliable economic statistics on the Somaliland economy are limited. However, based on a joint Ministry of Planning and World Bank initiative, a GDP estimate for 2012 (World Bank 2014) was approximated to be US$1.390 billion, excluding official development assistance (ODA). The largest sector was livestock with a 29.5 percent share of GDP, followed by wholesale and retail trade (19.5 percent), crops (8.2 percent), real estate activities (6.4 percent), forestry (5.2 percent), construction (3.7 percent), and information and communication (2.2 percent). In contrast, the GoS expenditures for 2013 as reported by the Ministry of Finance to the World Bank were US$115 million (So. Sh. 807 billion), financing public administration and defense sectors (3.4 percent of GDP) and partly financing education (2.7 percent of GDP) and health and social services (1.4 percent of GDP). Taxes and subsidies on products amounted to 6.7 percent of GDP in 2013. Also striking is the small size of the recordable financial sector, estimated at 0.3 percent of GDP, and the electricity and water supply sectors at 0.8 percent and 0.2 percent, respectively. Given these figures, it is little wonder that these are the sectors perceived to pose the greatest constraints to private sector development.

Firm Numbers and Size: The private sector in Somaliland comprises a wide cross section of larger-, medium-, small-, and micro-enterprises. This includes the largest companies in the telecommunications sector, such as Telesom, Telecom Somalia, Somtel, Africa Online, Nation Link, and Soltelco, and the remittance sector, which includes a further 20 firms and market leaders such as Dahabshiil, Salaama Bank, Amal Express, Kaah Express, and Qaran Express and leading trading companies such as Omaar Group. Business startup growth has been relatively robust, albeit from a very low base. While no definitive numbers can be provided, the current picture as of 2012 as provided by the MoCI showed a rapid increase between 2004 and 2010. The major activities were trade (including

wholesale and import/export enterprises), construction, and a smaller but significant number of business service enterprises. The growth in licenses is shown
in figure 2.1.

Licenses with the MoCI are in principle required by all enterprises. However,
in practice, only a very small proportion of enterprises do register with the
MoCI; a similarly limited number of enterprises are incorporated by the
Attorney General's Office under the Company's Act. Hence, these are not
representative sources of information. The most comprehensive data available
on the enterprise population are from the municipal license lists. Municipal
licenses are required for all enterprises occupying space in a given town (they
are in essence occupancy permits). The large majority of enterprises licensed
are retail outlets. The others listed include construction, hotels, and business
services. The current total of municipal licenses awarded in six main towns is
summarized in table 2.1.

Figure 2.1 Somaliland Growth in Business Licenses, 2004–10

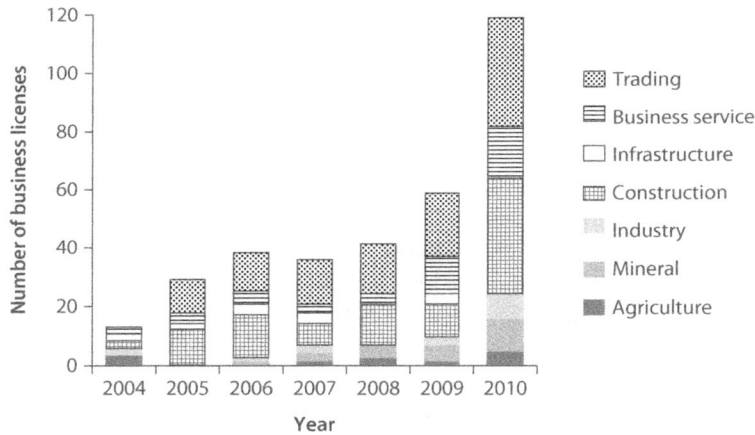

Table 2.1 Municipal Licenses, 2012

Town	Approx number of licenses
Hargeisa	7,500
Burao	4,200
Borama	1,200
Gobiley	600
Berbera	400
Sheik	200
Total	14,100

Source: Ministry of Commerce and Investment

Table 2.2 Licenses Issued by Category

Size category	Total licenses issued
1	108
2	767
3	1,612
4	1,415
5	3,450
6	2,789
7	662
N.A	2,455
Total	13,258

Source: Ministry of Commerce and Investment

The numbers of licenses are broken down into seven fee categories, which are based on expected turnover. This gives an approximate size categorization. Recent data for Hargeisa, also taken from municipal records, are shown in table 2.2.[2] The Hargeisa enterprise sector amounts to 13 registered businesses per thousand population. If this proportion was representative of the whole of Somaliland, it would rank about 50th out of a group of 83 economies.[3] The type of enterprises within each size category is mixed in terms of sector and therefore they cannot be sorted by type of activity.[4] The largest size category (tariff grade 1) includes banks; import and export; private (incorporated) enterprises; large hotels; supermarkets; large *khat* or *miraa* stores; mineral processing; vehicle retailers; and wholesale cigarette stores. At the other end of the scale, the smallest size category (tariff grade 7) includes small retail outlets (for example, food, clothing, books), repair shops (for example, shoes, tires, bicycles), and catering outlets (tea shops).

Principal Productive Sectors: Each of the leading production sectors in the Somaliland economy has its own distinct set of challenges and opportunities, political economy dynamics, and economic governance issues. In this section, some of the most pertinent aspects of three sectors are summarized.

Livestock: As noted above, livestock production accounts for almost 30 percent of Somaliland's GDP and is the single largest export. Roughly half of the population are pastoral and depend entirely on livestock production for their livelihood. Many more make a livelihood in the sale, transport, and export of livestock, or in processing livestock products in the domestic market. Anything that impacts livestock production has a major overall impact on the economy and especially on livelihoods. Unfortunately, the sector is not healthy.[5] Pastoralists face growing problems of access to viable rangeland due to a combination of enclosures, charcoal harvesting, and general environmental degradation. Veterinary services are mainly provided by the private sector and are unregulated, resulting in distribution and application of expired or inappropriate medicines. Somaliland livestock is smaller and in poorer condition than livestock from rival sources, such as Australia, and fetches a lower price. The entire value chain for livestock sales involves very marginal profit rates, except for the small number of mainly foreign firms engaged in exports. Most of the profits from the trade thus leave Somaliland. The sector's heavy dependence on the Saudi market for 80 percent of its exports reduces its options and bargaining position.

The sector's biggest vulnerabilities stem from market trends outside Somaliland. Goat and sheep consumption in the Gulf is declining due to competition from other meat products. Live animal exports are less attractive in the Gulf market except during the Haj seasons due to new preferences for prepared meat purchased in grocery stores. Exports are heavily concentrated during the Haj, which at times falls in seasons that are difficult for pastoralists. The livestock sector's stresses can be partly addressed with better government services and regulations—regulatory oversight of private veterinary services, better local markets, vigorous interventions to prevent illegal enclosures, charcoal harvesting, and other practices that contribute to rangeland degradation.

Fisheries:[6] The fishing sector is a resource in Somaliland with potential for increased domestic and export revenue, but it faces an array of major constraints. The Somaliland fisheries are not as abundant as those off the Puntland and the Republic of Yemen coasts, but an estimated 3,000 tons of fish are caught locally per year with an estimated potential catch of 180,000–200,000[7] tons of fish, 60 times the current levels of harvesting. Fish is not a desirable food product among Somalis, though consumption is growing, due—to a significant extent—to diaspora and international visitors. At present, domestic demand is outpacing supply. Fewer than 2,500 Somalilanders earn a livelihood as fishermen, most using rudimentary fishing equipment and small boats that cannot operate during the monsoon season (May–September). Inshore fisheries include an artisanal fleet of 100 active boats, as assessed in 2011. Exports of fish are currently limited to a few truckloads of frozen fish per month to Ethiopia. However, much more of the Somaliland catch is exported "off the books" via the Republic of Yemen. Nine industrial fishing vessels, all foreign, have secured licenses from the Somaliland government to fish in its waters.[8] Fish from the Somaliland coast are lost to foreign trawlers operating illegally out of Djibouti or coming from the Republic of Yemen, the Arab Republic of Egypt, Europe, and Asia.[9] As a result of legal technicalities, Somalia (and by extension Somaliland) is not formally registered in the Exclusive Economic Zone (EEZ), a sea zone within which countries have special sovereign rights. Until this is resolved, other countries can claim that their fishing vessels are not required to be licensed with the Somaliland government.

Expansion of fishing is hampered by a number of factors including lack of basic infrastructure in ports,[10] as well as inefficient processing, lack of market identification and promotion, and limited coordination among business associations. Moreover, limited training and skills result in hazardous and unhygienic fish handling, as well as a shortage of local capacity to repair equipment and vessels. The market for fish in Somaliland is largely undeveloped, with approximately 23 small markets in Hargesia for fish sales. Costs of fuel, ice, labor, and other inputs are higher in Somaliland than elsewhere such that local products struggle to compete with lower-priced substitute foods. Expansion of fishing for export is mainly hampered by quality and hygiene standards, which do not comply with international standards. In sum, current assessments indicate that the fishing sector value chain "exists at the most basic level and the needs are so fundamental that it is difficult to identify specific catalytic points in the chain where individual targeted interventions could have a transformative impact on the entire value chain." Most of the profit from domestic fish sales is captured by the small number of wholesalers—mainly eight local companies—that purchase or catch fish on the coast and truck the chilled fish to major urban markets in Hargeisa and Burao. Artisanal fishermen sell fish as low as US$0.07 a kilo to merchants, who resell at US$1.25 kilo in Hargeisa.[11]

Effective government regulation of and support to the fishing sector is limited by the very minimal resources of the Ministry of Fisheries (a budget of US$300,000 in 2014) and weak technical capacity. Steps that would need to be taken to allow the fishing sector to expand include greater government inspection capacity, support for cold chains, and more resources for coast guard patrols to reduce illegal fishing.

Horticulture—Gums and Resins:[12] Somaliland has long been a producer and exporter of gums and resins, harvested from wild trees indigenous to eastern Somaliland, mainly in the Sanaag region and parts of the Sool region. Four types of gums and resins are harvested; depending on the type of resin, they are used as thickeners, in fragrances, in chewing gum, and for aromatics. Although data on gums and resins production in Somaliland are not currently recorded by authorities, the total value of annual output is estimated at US$2.94 million. The value of exports of gums and resins reached US$2.1 million in 2009, with additional amounts probably exported unofficially to Ethiopia and Djibouti. Collection of the gums and resins is done by individual collectors, mainly poorer pastoralists, who dry and sort the gums before transporting them to Burao, where 10–15 major wholesalers operate. A price is negotiated after inspection. Collectors are said to have little bargaining power and earn so little for their work that many have left the business. After processing and grading, the gums and resins are sold to exporters.

Gums and resins exports have potential for growth, thanks to a large number of trees and high global demand. The sales history from 2003–10 of myrrh and *carteri* (frankincense) shows rising demand and prices since 2003 (see figure 2.2), but the sector faces a range of problems. They include chronic disputes over tree ownership, reflecting a broader problem of tenure and claims in rangeland areas that were once treated as common, overtapping of trees, labor shortage worsened by low prices offered to collectors, and very poor transport infrastructure in the

Figure 2.2 Demand and Pricing Trends for Myrrh and *Carteri,* 2003–10

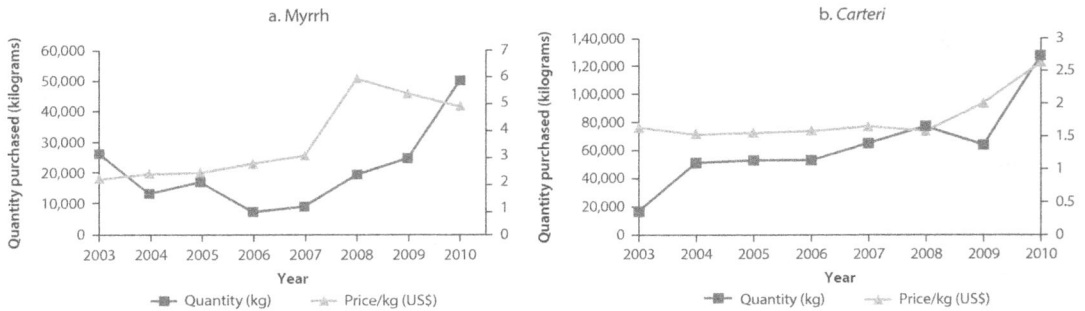

Source: GDS (2011, 26–27).

areas where gums and resins are tapped. Tensions between wholesalers and collectors over prices offered for gums and resins have clan implications, as the wholesalers tend to be from one Isaaq subclan, while collectors are mainly from clans in eastern Somaliland that have been split over affiliation with Somaliland. Moreover, the value chain structure is poorly organized, with several producer, exporter, and trader associations in existence but little horizontal or vertical integration. The sector also suffers from lack of uniform quality standards (for example, there is no system of traceability and controls), as well as improper sorting and grading.

Economic governance issues emerging from the political economy of the gums and resins subsector include the need for greater government regulation of wholesalers to ensure no collusion takes place, artificially driving down offering prices for gums and resins; legislation designed to address mounting problems of land tenure in rural areas; and improvement of transportation infrastructure in eastern Somaliland.

The Enabling Environment for Business

Taking a look at the private sector, based on the *Doing Business in Hargeisa 2012* report, which measures business regulations and enforcement, Hargeisa ranks 174 out of 183 economies on the ease of doing business. The ranking is an aggregate of 10 standardized indicators that examine business regulations as they apply to a domestic company throughout its life cycle (see figure 2.3). Hargeisa ranks highest (above other fragile and conflict-affected states—FCS) on dealing with construction permits, getting electricity, and registering property, but lowest on getting credit, protecting investors, resolving insolvency, and starting a business. Hargeisa's low ranking is due to several factors, including an incomplete legal and regulatory framework and overly burdensome administrative procedures. Additionally, costs in Hargeisa are high (including costs for business registration and tariff rates for water, sewage, and electricity), and there is low compliance with regulations.

Although Hargeisa ranks above average for Sub-Saharan Africa on dealing with construction permits, getting electricity, and registering property, the

Figure 2.3 Hargeisa's Performance on the *Doing Business* Indicators Compared with Sub-Saharan African Economies and Fragile and Conflict-affected States

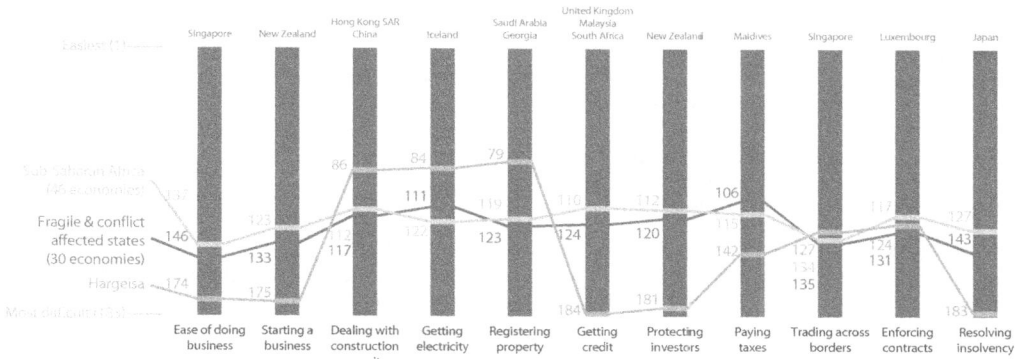

Source: World Bank and IFC 2012.

aggregate rankings belie details on cost and regulation. For example, on dealing with construction permits the indicator records the procedures, time, and cost required for a construction business to obtain all the necessary approvals to build a simple commercial warehouse and connect it to water, sewerage, and a fixed telephone. Hargeisa comes out above the average for Sub-Saharan Africa mainly because it is much faster than most countries (requiring 15 procedures and taking 56 days); however, the cost is much higher than in other countries, requiring US$1,038.80 of income per capita (compared to an average of US$823.70 of income per capita in Sub-Saharan Africa). This would place Hargeisa among the top 20 most costly economies, globally.

On "getting electricity," the indicator measures the procedures, time, and cost required for a small- to medium-sized enterprise to obtain a new electricity connection for a standardized warehouse with specific electricity needs (the subscribed capacity of the connection is 140 kilovolt amperes and the length of connection is 150 meters). Although Hargeisa's average is more than twice as fast and three times less expensive than the average for Sub-Saharan Africa, there is no regulatory framework or central authority overseeing power generation, distribution, and transmission and, as such, the process for obtaining an electricity connection is unregulated with regard to safety, technical standards, and procurement practices. The speed at which the external connection works are carried out is partly due to a lack of safety requirements and other technical standards, and the kilowatt per hour price of electricity—at US$0.80–1.00—is one of the highest in the world. Lastly, regarding "registering property," which measures the procedures necessary for a business to purchase a property and to transfer the property title to the buyer's name, the land registration system is still being rebuilt and remains largely incomplete. Moreover, there is no system for nonencumbrance verification to ensure that a property is free of charges and liens, which increases the probability of land conflicts.

Table 2.3 *Doing Business*'s "What to Reform"

Starting a business	Dealing with construction permits
• Reduce or abolish the paid-in minimum capital requirement • Clarify business classifications and consider reducing the cost of licensing • Streamline procedures and establish a one-stop shop for business start-up • Improve access to information and ensure transparency • Make it optional to use professional intermediaries and register with the Chamber of Commerce	• Draft and ratify a building code • Introduce inspection guidelines based on the risk characteristics of building • Establish a single access point for building permit clearances • Improve water sewerage infrastructure
Getting Electricity	**Registering Property**
• Adopt and implement an electricity regulatory framework • Introduce safety standards and supervision mechanisms for internal wiring • Increase the transparency of connection costs and processes	• Consider moving to a title-based system • Update the system of property rights registration • Coordinate the paper-based property registry and the GIS Office • Streamline fee payment procedures • Consider replacing percentage-based fees with fixed fees
Getting credit	**Protecting investors**
• Promote a system to exchange credit information • Enact a single comprehensive law concerning the use of movable assets as collateral • Implement a system of registration of movable property with a collateral registry	• Increase disclosure obligations to the board of directors and in the annual report • Involve shareholders in the approval of related party transactions • Make directors accountable for their actions • Grant shareholders greater access to corporate documents before and during trial • Make the companies law available in Somali
Paying taxes	**Trading across borders**
• Educate entrepreneurs and train accountants on the taxation system • Launch a communications campaign to raise awareness and diffuse potential resistance • Adopt accounting standards and develop tax regulation • Ensure transparency and consistency in the implementation of the tax system	• Streamline document requirements and make information publicly available • Improve roads to speed inland transportation and invest in port infrastructure • Computerize customs management and move towards exchanging trade information electronically
Enforcing contracts	**Resolving insolvency**
• Make laws available in Somali and publish court fee schedules • Train legal professionals and introduce specialization among judges • Keep performance statistics	• Increase confidence in the insolvency framework • Revise insolvency legislation to conform to international leading practices and introduce reorganization provisions • Train insolvency practitioners • Consider adopting guidelines that facilitate out-of-court workouts

Source: 2012 Doing Business in Hargeisa Report.

The *Doing Business* report lists a wide range of possible policy actions that could improve the business environment. These are summarized in table 2.3. Similarly, findings of a USAID-supported Business Confidence Index[13] identified the main challenges faced by enterprises as (a) lack of credit; (b) high energy costs; (c) shortage of skilled labor; (d) unreliable supply of materials; (e) tax burdens; (f) import competition; (g) property rights; (h) uncertain contract enforcement; and (i) poor roads. Finally, another perspective on the legal and regulatory environment is the Somaliland Investors Guide,[14] which describes the legal and regulatory framework for business as still under development and states that land records are incomplete and title search is difficult.

Societal and Cultural Assets

A discussion of the private sector in Somaliland cannot be concluded without consideration of the social and cultural capital that Somalilanders bring to their economic dealings, a key element of the resilience and success achieved to date by the private sector. Business owners in Somaliland consistently credit the region's peace and culture as major economic assets. Somaliland enjoys a level of peace and trust that allow businesses and individuals to settle disputes and manage affairs despite the limitations of the central government and judiciary. The enterprise survey (ES) provides some further insight into what is, given the insecurity of the Horn of Africa and sovereign limitations of the GoS, an achievement for which Somaliland's citizens and its government can rightly feel proud.

Consider the issue of trust. The ES results indicate that *the level of trust among Somalilanders is reasonably high, but it takes time and familiarity to build that trust.* The respondents were asked a number of questions regarding their level of trust with work colleagues, people who work in the stores in which they shop, people in general and the police and the media. Figure 2.4 provides a glimpse of the level of trust in Somaliland: a majority of respondents have "a lot" or "somewhat" level of trust in most of the areas covered and relatively few respondents showed no trust at all or only a little. For example, 69 percent of the respondents said that their level of trust in the people they work with is "a lot" and another 19 percent said it was "somewhat"; only 6.4 percent of the respondents chose no trust at all ("not at all"). For some of the cases depicted in figure 2.4, there is a significantly higher level of trust among micro and small firms relative to large firms; there is also some variation in the level of trust across the various regions of Somaliland. While female-owned firms report greater caution and distrust in their business partners and neighbors than other firms, female-owned firms also report more concerns about safety, potential violence, and gunfire in their communities.

A couple of other points stand out in figure 2.4. First, the level of trust in the police is high but not in the media. Second, the level of trust that the government will do its job with respect to enforcing certain criminal penalties is also high. Over 96 percent of firms responded that it is likely or highly likely that authorities would enforce the law if they committed a serious crime. Likewise, over 90 percent of firms believed the authorities would enforce the law if they failed to pay taxes on some of their income, and 84 percent believed they would be prosecuted if they obtained water or electrical services without

Figure 2.4 Trust Level Is High among People Who Frequently Interact But Not among the Rest

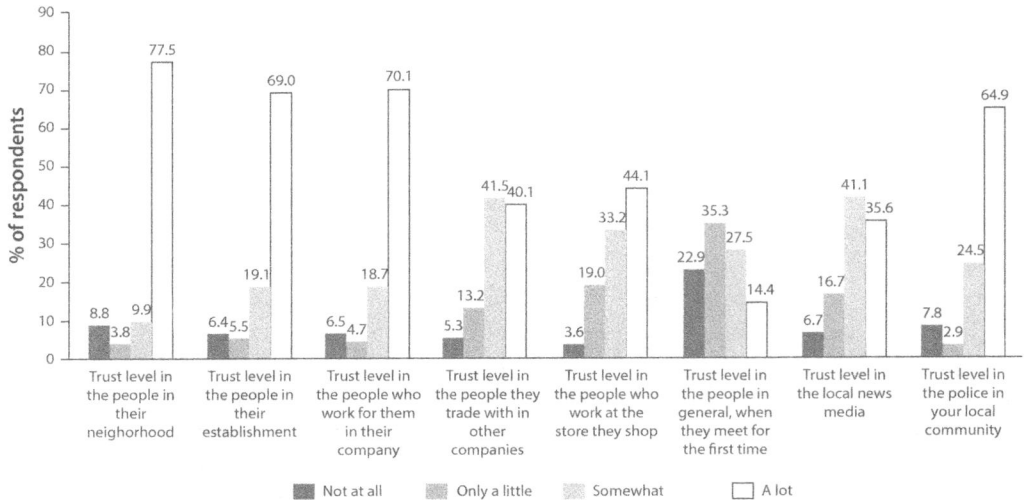

Source: Enterprise Surveys.

paying. However, there were areas of criticism. For instance, in discussions with private sector stakeholders, it was remarked that firms often do not know ahead of time how much they will pay at customs and the tariff rate that will be applied. This uncertainty may lead both to market inefficiencies and to distrust between businesses and government. For the diaspora, who must manage their investments from a distance and where local competitors have more familiarity with the business environment, trust is a major factor influencing business transactions. Given the weaknesses in the business environment, including dispute resolution mechanisms, investors must rely heavily on local partners to monitor activities on the ground. Choosing the right individuals for business partnership is therefore critical. Diaspora consultations revealed a general tendency for investors, when they are not working with family members, to reach out to only a limited number of carefully selected partners. This tends to depress investment activity.

Crime is another important indicator of social cohesion. The level of crime in Somaliland is low, which is in contrast to many FCS countries that were not able to demobilize and integrate combatants as effectively as was done in Somaliland. The ES results showed that *the respondents feel relatively safe in their neighborhoods.* The ES provides information on the actual experiences of firms with crime incidents and spending on security as well as the opinions of the respondents (managers/owners) about various aspects related to the security situation. These data seem to suggest that while the crime situation is favorable in Somaliland, individuals and firms are concerned enough to take precautionary measures. Specifically, during 2012, about 7.5 percent of the firms in Somaliland experienced losses due to crime. Compared with this finding, the corresponding figure for the comparator countries is significantly higher at 15 percent. Within Somaliland, there is some variation in the level of crime across regions. For example, about 34 percent of the firms in Borama reported losses due to crime compared with no firm reporting such losses in Wajaale. However, not much difference is found between other firm types distinguished by size or sector.

Given the relatively low levels of crime incidents, it is not surprising that respondents have a favorable opinion about the security situation in Somaliland (figure 2.5). For example, when the owners or managers were asked if they feel they are likely to be victims of crime in the next 12 months, 84 percent either disagreed or strongly disagreed with such a possibility. Figure 2.5 shows qualitatively similar results for some of the other perception-related questions. Perception of how favorable the security situation is does show some variation within Somaliland, for example, between small and large cities. For example, only about 1 percent of respondents in the large cities strongly disagreed with feeling safe from crime and violence while at home compared with a significantly higher figure of 9 percent in the small cities.

Despite the low level of crime and the favorable opinions about security discussed above, about 73 percent of the firms in the full sample paid for security during the last year. Such spending is more common among large firms (88 percent) compared with micro (67 percent) and small firms (76 percent). Nonetheless, only 2.4 percent of respondents cited crime, theft, and disorder as a major constraint to running their businesses. Similarly, 75 percent of the respondents in the full sample stated that they avoid certain ways and areas that they think are dangerous. In addition, about 55 percent of the respondents reported hearing gunshots in their neighborhood and close to 24 percent believe that the level of crime has increased in Somaliland over the

Figure 2.5 Opinions about the Security Situation in Somaliland Are Mostly Favorable

Source: Enterprise Surveys.

last two years. These results suggest that while the crime situation in Somaliland is not bad, it is not an issue about which there is any room for complacency.

Notwithstanding the clearly significant and positive force that Somaliland's form of social capital has played in fostering private sector growth, it also has inherent limits. These limits can inhibit economic growth, economic diversification, and the opening up to regional and international markets that can bring improved living standards to Somaliland. For example, during the diaspora meetings, there was a sentiment that a more conventional and transparent rules-based system, rather than one based on informal social capital, needs to be in place if more market and larger resource-seeking, rather than strategic (that is, real estate) investment is to be attracted. As seen earlier, the *Doing Business* report makes a number of recommendations as to legal, policy, and administrative reforms to be pursued in furtherance of a more formal institutional framework for business activity that would serve to improve private sector performance.

Current Initiatives in Private Sector Development

In support of the SNDP, a number of private sector development initiatives have been under way in Somaliland, supported by the international community. This includes the recently concluded U.S. Agency for International Development (USAID) "Partnership for Economic Growth," as well as ongoing work of the Food and Agriculture Organization (FAO), the International Labour Organization (ILO), and the United Nations Development Programme (UNDP).

The World Bank, in collaboration with the United Kingdom (UK) Department for International Development (DFID) and the Danish International Development Agency (DANIDA), is in the final stages of a four-year project (SomPREP II). The project strives to address constraints to enterprise start-up and financing and have the promise of relatively shorter-term outcomes. Other aspects of the program, such as support for financial sector supervision, development of infrastructure through public–private partnerships (PPPs), and development of targeted value chains, entail outcomes requiring even longer lead times before measurable results can be reliably ascertained. Box 2.1 summarizes the components and some of the results and outputs to date of the SomPREP II initiative.

While it is too early to determine the net effect of these initiatives on the longer-term prospects for private sector development, this is a time-bound initiative that provides—at best—effective transitory support to what is a larger institutional development and financial sector inclusion challenge. This will entail a reform agenda that places considerable capacity burden on a stretched government and requires long-term sustained support. This can only come if accompanied by clear-cut definitive policy outcome milestones that only the government can deliver. The goal is to have international support more directly

Box 2.1 Somalia PSD Re-engagement Phase II Project

The Somalia Private Sector Development Re-engagement Phase II Project (US$24.5million) is a 2011–15 World Bank program targeting interventions mostly in Somaliland. The project is the first World Bank intervention to target the rebuilding of the private sector since the 1991 civil war in Somalia. SomPrepII focuses on strengthening the competitiveness and capacity of the private sector to catalyze investment and create jobs. The project development objectives are to improve access to markets and generate employment in key productive and services sectors. The project's multidonor trust fund is supported by DANIDA, DFID, and the World Bank's State and Peacebuilding Fund (SPF) and covers five major areas of support.

Investment Climate

The "one-stop shop" for business registration is designed to improve the investment climate for Somaliland by reducing the time and cost of starting and operating a formal business through the introduction of pilot One Stop Shops (OSS) for business registration. In 2013, the OSS team conducted a legal and institutional assessment of enterprise registration and licensing, and technical and institutional solutions were agreed with the government for the establishment of three one-stop business facilitation centers in Hargeisa, Berbera, and Burao. In addition, the team conducted reviews of the Companies Act and Commercial Licensing Act and developed a draft new company law for government consideration. The pilot centers have been established with an initial target of registering 500 new businesses.

Financial Sector

The financial sector component focuses on strengthening the bank supervision legal framework consistent with international standards and best practices to support commercial banking. Although the Banking, Credit and Financial Institutions (BCFI) bill—a crucial piece of the legal framework to support banking in Somaliland—has not been passed, World Bank activities have focused on the development of a transitional bank and financial institution licensing supervision framework, and the development of a banking supervision unit.

Gums and Resins and Fisheries Value Chains

Support to the gums and resins and fisheries sectors targets improvements in operational capacity of the private sector, as well as capacity of the government and business associations to support the industries. Activities under the gums and resins sector have focused on improving processing and packaging of the product for export and the design and implementation of an international marketing and branding program, as well as advisory support to the Ministry of Environment, specifically on a management information system intended to capture price, quantity, and export value data on gums and resins. Activities under the fisheries sector have included direct training to fisherman to improve their fishing techniques, a stocktaking of fisheries associations and fisherman vessels, development of a fish awareness campaign focusing on the benefits of consuming fish, as well as support to the Ministry of Fisheries on quality control. In 2013 the number of active fishing vessels in Berbera increased from 40 to 90, employing 450 fishermen. Ice production has increased by

box continues next page

Box 2.1   Somalia PSD Reengagement Phase II Project *(continued)*

136 percent, and the number of producers has increased from 2 to 5, leading to a drop in the price of ice by one-third. Moreover, the value of the total catch increased from US$3.8 million to US$8.6 million.

PPP—Ports and Solid Waste

The objective of the public–private partnership component of the project is to improve the enabling environment for investment, services expansion, and quality improvements in private provision of selected port services and solid waste management. Under the port sector, the project produced a comprehensive strategic economic assessment of the Port of Berbera. The work included an extensive stakeholder dialogue process that resulted in an agreement and a formal government request to the World Bank to pursue and implement a PPP project in marine and cargo handling. Under the solid waste sector, support has focused on providing advisory support to solid waste contractors in Hargesia for the collection of waste and advisory assistance to the Municipality of Hargeisa and Solid Waste Management Association. A significant milestone was reached through the ratification of the Municipal Solid Waste (MSW) policy, Framework for PPP contracts and MSW bylaws. These documents provide the necessary institutional instruments to guide waste collection and disposal operations and to regulate MSW services in the City of Hargeisa.

Somaliland Business Fund

The Somaliland Business Fund (SBF) is a US$10 million matching grant scheme managed by the World Bank designed to provide direct support to the private sector to promote enterprise start-up and growth to create sustainable employment and income opportunities. The SBF is an open, competitive scheme that cofinances business development services as well as physical and capital assets on a matching basis (from 50 to 66 percent of the total investment). The project approved a first round of 80 grants (59 small and 21 large) in March and June 2013, valued at $4.65 million and employing an anticipated 1,323 workers (of which an estimated 488 were jobs for women). The second round of awards were made in June 2014 for 95 grants (74 small and 21 large grants) valued at $6.35 million, employing a projected 1,444 workers (of which an estimated 506 were jobs for women). The subsector spread of grants under the program was diverse, with a focus on livestock, fisheries, alternative energy and manufacturing.

support endogenous institutional development and private sector investment, rather than just compensate for its absence or insufficiency. But the framework for this type of international support to be provided is substantively not yet in place.

In view of this, the following chapters seek to identify the most significant constraints and make recommendations as to where the government should focus its attention in terms of policy and programming options in the enterprise sector, the financial sector, and government.

Notes

1. For more on Somali customary law and informal contracts, see Lewis (2002), Gundel (2006), and LeSage (2005).

2. Grade 1 is the largest size category and attracts the highest license fee (approximately US$200 a year), while grade 7, the smallest, attracts about US$20 a year at the current informal exchange rate. The data collected from different sources are not consistent and are yet to be finalized.

3. Somaliland—while a self-declared independent state—has not been formally recognized by the international community, and as such remains for legal purposes a subsovereign territory within Somalia. Nevertheless, the term "Somaliland" is used throughout this report. World Development Indicator Database and Nationmaster. com. Cited in World Bank (2012).

4. The International Labour Organization has recommended a sector-based categorization of fee grades.

5. The following assessment of the sector draws on data generated in DAI (2011, 49–126) and GDS (2011).

6. Observations on the fishery sector are derived from a combination of interviews, site visits to fish processing plants, and data compiled in DAI (2011, 127–50) and GDS (2011).

7. This reference is taken from FAO.

8. DAI (2011) reports that these licenses were issued for US$50,000 apiece, dating back to 2005.

9. According to one interview, 40 percent of all of the Republic of Yemen's fish catch is from Somaliland or Somali territorial waters.

10. Much-needed improvements in basic infrastructure include dredging the Berbera and Seylac ports, rehabilitating the jetties for access by artisanal fishermen, and providing cold storage; Mait lacks a dock or jetty.

11. DAI (2011, 143). The Somaliland fish market is "undiscerning," meaning all fish regardless of species and quality tend to be priced the same.

12. Data on which this assessment is based were derived from field interviews, from DAI (2011, 1992–96).

13. As developed under the USAID "Partnership for Economic Growth" project.

14. Somaliland Investors Guide (USAID).

CHAPTER 3

Enterprise Performance

The Somaliland economy has a hugely valuable asset in its innovative and pragmatic population and culture, which has allowed Somaliland to make significant strides since the civil war. However, other evidence from the enterprise surveys (ESs), diaspora dialogue, and consultations with stakeholders shows that this asset is becoming increasingly overburdened as the economy has begun to outgrow the informal institutions supporting it until now. The degree to which this is an underregulated economy is measured to an extent by the *2012 Doing Business* report, which reveals a business sector in Somaliland with some of the most fundamental enabling environment challenges including business start-up, access to factor markets, investor protection, efficient dispute resolution, and ease of exit (insolvency resolution).

It is also important to note that there needs to be the right balance of regulation to ensure that the public sector does not place too heavy a footprint on the private sector in its concern to create a more predictable, transparent, and formally rules-based business environment. Getting this balance right will entail a range of considerations. Given the GoS objectives of growth and employment creation, evidence on enterprise performance and its most pressing constraints will serve to highlight areas where policy initiatives could be focused to achieve some early progress on these twin objectives. This includes where to address regulatory and promotional efforts.

Sales and Jobs

The ES for Somaliland provides information on total annual sales of firms for 2012 and 2010. Using these data, sales growth was computed as the difference in annual sales between these two years, divided by the average level of sales in the two years (Haltiwanger growth formula). Information is also available on total wages and benefits paid to workers (henceforth, payroll) during 2012 and 2010. The growth rate in payroll is computed similarly to sales growth and is used as a proxy for job creation.[1]

On Sales Growth: The median sales growth rate in Somaliland equals 10 percent (per annum) and the mean value is 13.8 percent. There is a strong and significant correlation between sales growth rate and a number of variables related to the structure of the firm, level of competition, gender composition of the owners, and the level of security and trust as perceived by the firms. Sales growth is strongly and inversely correlated with the initial level of sales (annual sales in 2010). That is, there is strong convergence, with initially large firms growing more slowly than small firms. For example, firms in the bottom decile by initial sales experienced a median growth rate of 20 percent per annum compared with a median growth rate of just 9 percent for firms in the top decile. Since firm size tends to be correlated with a number of firm characteristics, it is not surprising that some of the covariates of growth rate lose their significance after controlling for initial sales. However, some correlations do survive the control for initial sales, as discussed below.

Growth in sales is higher among firms with more educated management. Close to 14 percent of the surveyed firms have a top decision maker who has either no education or primary education but not higher. As might be expected, sales growth is significantly lower among firms with managers having no or only primary schooling (a mean growth rate of 5.5 percent per annum) compared with firms with more educated managers (a mean growth rate of 16.9 percent per annum).

Faster-growing firms seem to have a worse perception of enforcement of laws than slower-growing firms. Firms were asked how likely they think the law would be enforced if a crime were committed, if taxes were not paid, or if someone took household services (water and electricity) without paying. For two of these three enforcement questions (nonpayment of taxes and obtaining household services without payment), firms reporting very likely (as opposed to less likely) show a much slower growth rate than the rest. For example, sales growth for firms reporting nonpayment of taxes as very likely to invite enforcement of the law equals 7.7 percent compared with a much higher growth rate of 22 percent for firms that consider the enforcement to be just likely, not very likely, or not at all likely. One possible explanation is that the faster-growing firms are more likely to benefit from better enforcement and hence are more likely to complain about existing lax tax enforcement. It should be noted that female-owned firms tend to be less convinced that laws will be enforced fairly. This suggests there could be a unevenness in the government treatment of higher versus lower growing firms.

On Payroll Growth: The median growth rate in payrolls is 16 percent (per annum)and the mean growth rate is 29 percent. Results for growth rate in payrolls show only a few robust correlations with various firm characteristics. Much like sales growth rate, payrolls also show a convergence effect. That is, the growth rate in payrolls is significantly and inversely correlated with the initial (year 2010) value of total payrolls. Payrolls growth rate is also significantly inversely correlated with the initial (year 2010) value of annual sales (log values).

Here again there is a systematic difference between old and young firms—the growth rate is much higher for relatively young firms, and this result holds even after controlling for the initial level of payrolls. For example, estimation results show that moving from the 25th to the 75th percentile value of age (from 6 to 16 years) in Somaliland is associated with a decrease in payrolls growth rate of about 15.8 percentage points. This is an economically large change, given that the mean value of payrolls growth rate equals 29 percent in the sample.

To further understand factors that might be at play in employment, firms were asked about their recruiting methods; that is whether during the last year the firm found new employees through the following channels: family and friends; word of mouth; public advertisement; and the residual category of other channels. *Growth rate of payrolls is significantly lower for firms that used the more traditional channels of family and friends and word of mouth than those that did not use these channels.* For example, firms using family and friends show a growth rate in payrolls of 20 percent compared with a significantly higher growth rate of 32 percent for firms that did not use family and friends.

Key Enterprise Constraints

Whereas the *Doing Business* assessment provides a picture of the supply side of government services, the ES provides more insight into how this "supply" impacts firm performance. As can be seen from figure 3.1, a pronounced lack of access to finance, poor infrastructure services (transport, electricity, water), a lack of clarity regarding land titling and dispute resolution, a wide-ranging shortage of desired skills among the workforce, and a lack of incentives to move into the formal sector are significant causal factors, according to the firms themselves. Each of these issues is addressed in turn.

Access to Finance

When asked to choose the single most important or biggest obstacle to their business from a list of 16 obstacles, *poor access to finance was the most commonly chosen obstacle* (by 49 percent of the firms) followed by access to land (by 25 percent of the firms).

The survey indicates that while roughly one-third of businesses had an outstanding loan at the end of 2012, less than 2 percent of businesses applied for a loan or line of credit during the 2012 fiscal year. Even more telling, of the 98 percent of firms that did not apply for a loan in 2012, only 6.5 percent reported that they did not have need for a loan. Follow-up discussions with business owners confirmed that the use of financial services is constrained by a number of factors. Financial services such as loans and lines of credit are not available formally in Somaliland and therefore the number of firms that apply for loans or lines of credit is limited primarily to those that have access to foreign credit

Figure 3.1 Access to Finance Is the Most Commonly Chosen Single Most Important Obstacle by Firms in Somaliland

■ % of firms reporting the biggest obstacle to their business

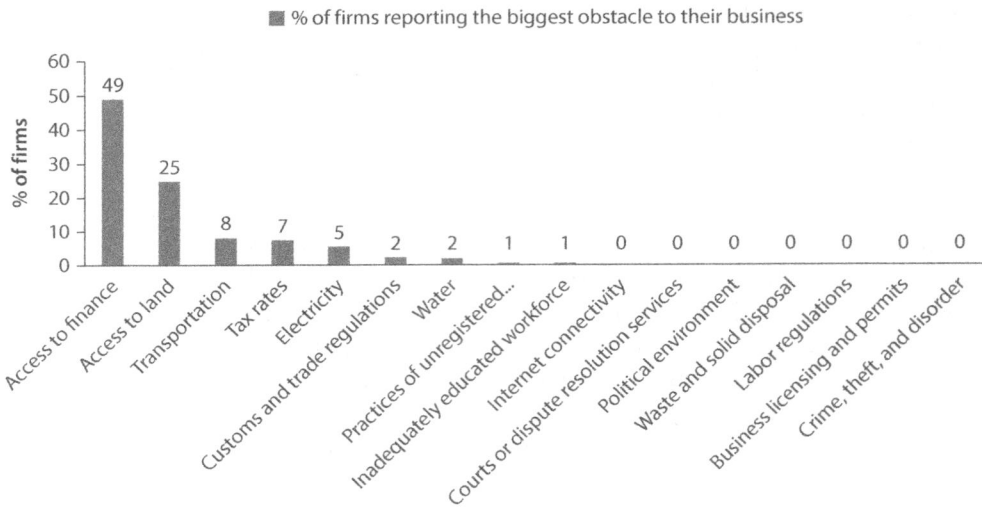

Source: Enterprise Surveys.

Box 3.1 Why Does Access to Finance Matter?

Studies show that finance is important for economic development and firm growth. The availability of external finance is positively associated with entrepreneurship and higher firm entry as well as with firm dynamism and innovation (Aghion, Fally, and Scarpetta 2007).

Finance also allows existing firms to exploit growth and investment opportunities and to achieve larger equilibrium size (Raja and Zingales 1998; Beck et al. 2005). In addition, firms can safely acquire a more efficient productive asset portfolio where the institutional and regulatory frameworks for finance are in place, and firms are also able to choose more efficient organizational forms such as incorporation (Claessens and Laeven 2003; Demirguc-Kunt et al. 2006).

Finally, this line of research has shown that the impact of financial sector deepening on firm performance and growth is stronger for small- and medium-sized firms than for large enterprises (Beck et al. 2005, 2008). Levine (2005) provides a good overview of the related literature.

---

markets or loans from friends and family. In Somaliland, the proportion of firms reporting access to finance as the biggest obstacle does not vary much either by firm size or female participation in ownership; small versus large cities are also roughly similar in this regard.

Access to finance is also a major obstacle for the diaspora. During the diaspora consultations, investors confirmed that they rely primarily on personal savings and/or borrowing from family members or business partners to support commercial investment in Somaliland. Some of the investors interviewed, who had failed businesses, cited lack of access to capital as a main reason why they were unsuccessful. Although some diaspora investors confirmed that they had access to credit in the countries where they lived, many explained that it was difficult to obtain financing for projects either because they had difficulty meeting the requirements to borrow or they could not obtain financing to invest overseas. Insurance to cover basic business risks is also unavailable in Somaliland. Thus, investors noted that they operated in highly unpredictable environments with no assistance in the event of a natural disaster or property damage. The contribution of diaspora financing to Somaliland's economy is significant;[2] therefore, limitations on access to finance for diaspora have implications for the economy as a whole.

Among household-based businesses (HBB), access to finance is the second most commonly cited obstacle behind access to water. This may reflect several factors, including the type of businesses that tend to be household based and the fact that HBBs tend to be served by micro-finance institutions in the sample. For example, compared to the more formal enterprises, HBBs are much more likely to have or use external sources of finance such as micro-finance institutions (51 percent of HBBs vs. 0.5 percent of enterprises), while the opposite holds true regarding the use of formal savings accounts (44 percent of HBBs vs. 77 percent of more formal enterprises).[3]

Reasons for not applying for a loan also show sharp difference between formal firms and HBBs. Within the sample of firms that did not apply for a loan during 2012, the main reason for not applying is illustrated in the following statistic. Having "no need for a loan" was the main reason for not applying for a loan for 66 percent of HBBs but only 6.5 percent of the formal firms. These differences suggest that varied policy responses are required for improving access to finance for formal firms and HBBs. Female-owned firms are, however, more likely to have borrowed money from informal sources such as friends and family than male-owned firms.

Electricity

Electricity costs are roughly US$1 per kilowatt hour leaving most (~65 percent) micro-enterprises and HBBs without access to electricity. In fact, HBBs are four times less likely to own a generator and nearly 20 percent less likely to have access to a private electricity source. Eighty-two percent of firms in Berbera are served by public electric utilities. But this is the exception. Only 13 percent of firms in Hargeisa get electricity from public sources, while the remainder of the businesses in Somaliland rely entirely on private sources for electricity, mostly in the form of diesel generators. Firms cite relatively infrequent power outages—only four per month for a total of 8.8 hours of outage in a typical month (note that regular scheduled outages, load shedding, and changeover were not counted in this figure). This may not reflect the full nature of the constraints posed by electricity, as firms may compensate by adjusting expectations and operating in low electricity-intensive industries. Improvements in electricity infrastructure would

Box 3.2 Why Does Access to Infrastructure Matter?

Over the last two decades, a large body of literature has analyzed the economic impact of infrastructure services on economic outcomes, with mixed results.

These effects differ across sectors and regions. Dollar, Hallward-Driemeier, and Mengistae (2005), using survey data from Bangladesh, China, India, and Pakistan, found that even after controlling for firm characteristics and region- or country-level effects, power losses have a significantly negative effect on total factor productivity. Aterido and Hallward-Driemeier (2007) carried out a related study with particular focus on Africa. In this case, a higher incidence of power outages is shown to most negatively impact employment growth. Not only does electricity have large effects on firm productivity (Straub 2008), economic development (Lipscomb, Mobarak, and Barham 2013; and others), and employment, but evidence suggests that its availability can also have a significant impact on female employment. (Dinkelman 2011).[4]

There is evidence also that infrastructure in general explains 9 percent of firm-level productivity, which is the second highest percentage after red tape, corruption, and crime in Escribano and Guasch (2005). In this careful econometric study using Guatemala, Honduras, and Nicaragua survey data, various productivity measures were regressed on infrastructure variables, with findings demonstrating significant effects of power outages, transportation losses, and Internet access on productivity.

have significant positive economic development impacts. Efforts to encourage the development of safe, reliable, and less expensive energy should be a priority for fostering economic growth because of its potential effects both on quantity of economic activity and on the scope of viable businesses that can thrive with improved electrical access.

Access to land

Land titling, registration, and formalization take place largely at the local level in a piecemeal fashion. *While the vast majority of businesses have some documentation supporting the status of the land they occupy, a far smaller share feel confident that the documentation would be enforceable during a dispute.* Many business owners are concerned with transparency in the sale and registration processes for land. A lack of clarity in this area has significant effect on investment decisions, capital accumulation, formalization, resources expended in defending land rights, and productivity of businesses.[5] Common problems in Somaliland typically result from factors such as trespassing (mostly expanding fences into a neighbor's property), land enclosure of communal land resources, and fraudulent eviction (often the result of duplicate or forged landownership certificates).[6] Due to the lengthly time and cost of official court deliberations, most businesses prefer either customary resolution systems or local courts/dispute committees. That being said, while a large number of court cases (71 percent) in Hargeisa were still pending decisions in 2013, 28 percent of reported conflicts were decided through municipal courts and 1 percent of conflicts were resolved through out-of-court traditional mediation processes. In contrast in Burao in 2013, 40 percent of land disputes were resolved out of court, 35 percent were resolved by local government, and only 25 percent of disputes were settled through official court deliberations.[7]

Land was also discussed in every diaspora focus group meeting. Regarded as a relatively low-risk investment, land and real estate are the most common forms of investment for the diaspora (Hammond et al. 2011), although conflicts around land are common and prices have risen in the past 10 years due to speculation and land grabbing. In a baseline assessment of landownership, diaspora returnees were identified as the main victims of land conflict (the second most vulnerable group to land conflict after the poor).[8] Diaspora returnees may be particularly vulnerable to conflict because their records may have been lost or destroyed during the war. Moreover, for the diaspora who did not grow up in Somaliland or who left Somaliland for an extended period, lack of familiarly with the land allocation, transfer, and dispute resolution practices may make it more difficult to navigate through these processes.

In addition to the limitations currently impacting the transfer, registration, and procedures for addressing land disputes which are predominately a municipal responsibility, two additional factors are important for the effective economic deployment of land. First, land officially belongs to the "State" of Somaliland as stated in Article 12, paragraph 1 of the 1999 Constitution. The responsibility over all land management rests with the Ministry of Public Works, Housing and Transport (MoPWHT). One of the principal functions of the MoPWHT is to prepare master plans for land development and public purpose objectives. To date a viable master plan for Somaliland and its municipal centers has not been put into effect. Second, there has been no effective dialogue between the different ministries of central government and the municipal authorities to develop a strategic and coordinated approach to land zoning for economic development purposes such as the special economic zones, including industrial parks. To the extent that this has taken place, it has been on an *ad hoc* basis through parceling of land for specific usage by incumbents with ownership credentials in bilateral consultation principally with municipal authorities.

The establishment of a master plan, complemented by more effective interministerial and intergovernmental cooperation would serve to clarify priority legal, regulatory, and investment requirements and provide a much stronger basis to attract development financing in support of the master plan implementation.

Skills

While businesses are quite adept at introducing new goods and services to the market in Somaliland (see below for more discussion on firm innovation), skills shortages are a constantly mentioned constraint by business. This is apparent from the survey and the various interviews conducted during the consultation process. Developing workforce capacity to meet the current and future needs of businesses is an important issue at both the firm and economy levels. One important feature is mutual understanding of the skills and capabilities thought necessary for current and future business performance. *Skills shortages are widespread and cover every type of skills, from customer service to engineering and maintenance to management.* Many large businesses employ expatriates for the more highly skilled positions and often import technical, mechanical, and maintenance staff to service equipment. The need for improved vocational training opportunities is frequently cited by businesses. Female-owned businesses—which generally have a manager with less experience and workers with fewer years of education than male-owned firms—complain of skills shortages far more often than male-owned businesses.[9] It is worth noting in this context that managers in male-owned firms have nearly twice the experience (14.6 years) compared to managers in female-owned firms (8.5 years) and are nearly twice as likely to have completed secondary school.[10] A significant number of businesses also report difficulty in recruiting unskilled workers (see figure 3.2). Within these findings, tech-savvy businesses tend to be newer and smaller and report difficulty in hiring people with computer-related skills.

Diaspora investors are also impacted by the limited skill base in Somaliland. Discussions with diaspora investors confirmed that in many cases, basic skills and

Figure 3.2 Firms Experience Difficulty in Recruiting Workers in a Variety of Job Categories, Including Unskilled Labor

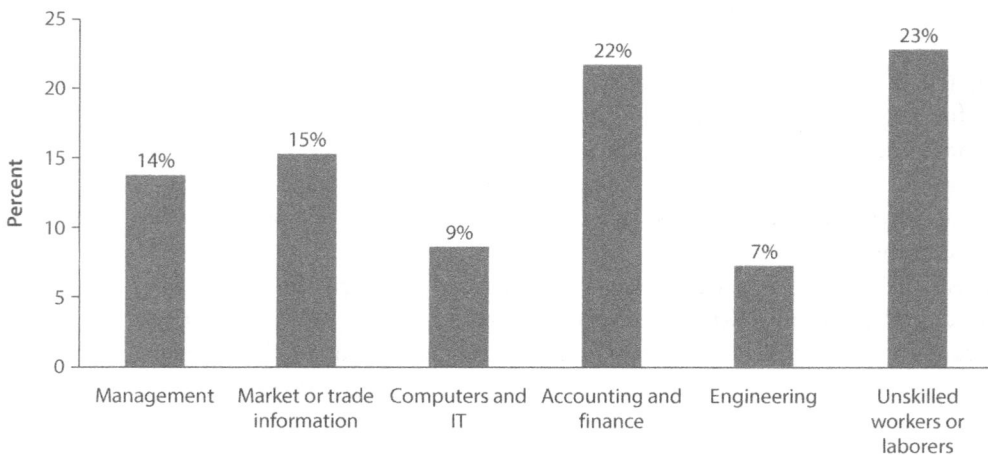

Source: World Bank enterprise survey.

sector-specific technical skills are lacking in the local environment, which can be a major deterrent for investing in Somaliland vis-à-vis other more attractive locations. Several investors confirmed that they hired foreign workers for reasons including better work ethic/ability to work a standard eight-hour day, a specialized skill that could not be found locally, and/or lower cost of labor. The diaspora interviewees confirmed that turnover tends to be high for most locally hired employees.

It is important to note that the discussion above relates to the *ranking* of obstacles. That is, how a given obstacle compares with other obstacles. This ranking does not necessarily have any correlation with the severity of the obstacle for firm operations on an absolute scale. For this reason, the ES also provides information on the absolute level of severity of the various obstacles. The percentage of firms that reported the obstacle as more than a minor obstacle (moderate, major, or very severe obstacle) largely mirrors the results from the ranking cited above and was highest for access to finance (75 percent), followed by access to land (72 percent), and electricity (47 percent).

Some Entry Points for New Employment

There is much that needs to be addressed if the enabling environment for the private sector is to experience a significant improvement and foster new investment for employment growth. The ES analysis does provide some important guidance as to where government's shorter- and longer-term focus should be directed. In the first place, those businesses more dependent on infrastructure—most commonly in manufacturing where production processes are most sensitive to the quality of power supplies and the movement of goods over longer distances to and from regional and international markets—face more intractable obstacles. Solutions entail policy actions and investment levels that will take time to put in place and need to be addressed over a medium- and longer-term horizon. Alternatively, there are entry points for more immediate results, particularly in the service sectors, pertaining to innovation-oriented and female-headed and/or primarily female-owned businesses. The ES analysis also raises the issue of firm start-up and formalization and the crucial importance of Berbera port. These four issues are addressed below.

Innovation
The survey findings show that innovation activity seems to be widespread in Somaliland in the sense that a majority of firms introduced a new product or service as well as new methods of manufacturing or delivering services over the last three years. Over the last three years, about 57 percent of the firms in Somaliland introduced a new product/service and 64 percent introduced a new method of manufacturing or offering services. In short, a majority of firms in Somaliland are involved in some kind of product and process innovation.[11] Further characteristics as presented in figure 3.3 are summarized below:

Figure 3.3 Innovation Activity in Somaliland

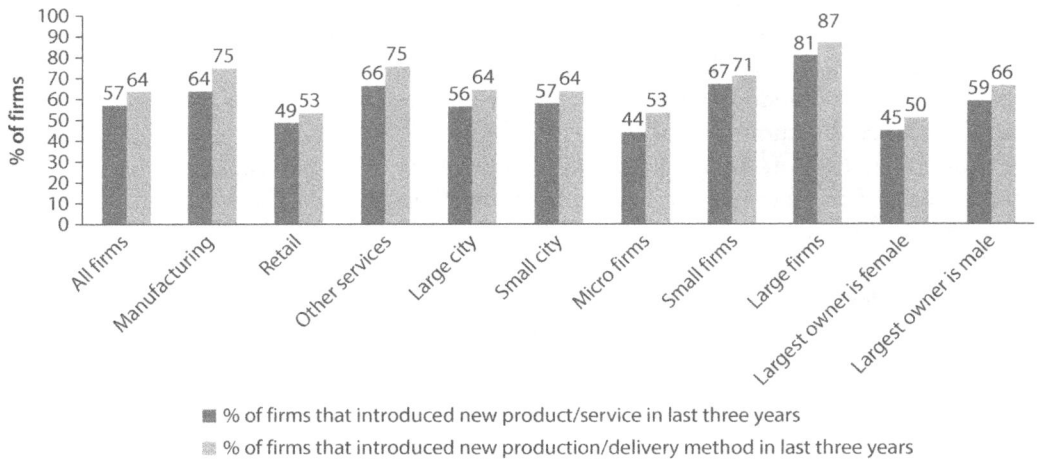

■ % of firms that introduced new product/service in last three years
▩ % of firms that introduced new production/delivery method in last three years

Source: Enterprise Surveys.

- The proportion of innovating firms is significantly higher among larger firms and in manufacturing and in service sectors other than retail.
- Specifically, over the last three years, only 54 percent of retail firms introduced an improved production or delivery method. This is notably lower than the corresponding figure of 75 percent for manufacturing firms and 75 percent for other services firms.
- Firms of all sizes and in all sectors innovated more through production process changes than the introduction of new products and services.
- The percentage of firms that introduced a new product or service in the last three years is also significantly lower among retail firms (49 percent) compared with other service sector firms (66 percent).[12]
- Controlling for firm size and compared with the rest of the firms, firms that introduced a new product or service in the last three years have higher labor productivity, a higher proportion of annual sales that are exported, a higher proportion of inputs that are imported, and are relatively older.

Innovating firms, specifically in the service sector, with higher productivity and sales performance, have less exposure to the larger infrastructure constraints. *They offer a high probability, shorter-term opportunity to create new jobs and market opportunities that provide additional indirect employment demand.* Their primary needs include finance, skilled labor, and market and technical information. Government and donor efforts could focus on identifying the different subsectors with a good track record of innovation and support businesses operating in these sectors to access these inputs.

Female-owned Businesses

Evidence in Somaliland strongly suggests that firms with women in top positions tend to have a higher proportion of female workers than other firms. One reason for this could be that women in top positions tend to open doors for other female workers. It is also possible that certain types of jobs or sectors that are more favorable to women tend to attract female managers and owners as well as employees. For either of the two or other reasons, the proportion of females in the workforce is significantly higher in Somaliland among firms with a female largest owner than a male largest owner (43 percent vs. 7 percent). The result holds separately for the sample of micro, small, and large firms and also for manufacturing, retail, and other service sectors, with the exception that large firms have a roughly similar percentage of female workers irrespective of the level of female ownership. Firms with female ownership are also far more likely to be formed as partnerships than male-owned firms. Discussions with a number of female business owners suggest that while females are not constrained in how they form businesses either by laws or by social norms; they are often constrained by costs and family responsibilities. Partnerships allow women to share the costs, risks, and responsibilities associated with starting and running a business by pooling resources.

Regardless of the reasons why women tend to work for and with other women, it is important to note that *female-owned businesses in Somaliland are the primary driver of female employment in the economy and are therefore critical to the wellbeing of women in Somaliland. Improving female participation in economic activity is important not only for improving the economic condition of women but also for overall economic development and growth.* To strengthen female involvement in the market and in enterprises, particular attention needs to be paid to correct for distortions that impact their productivity. For instance sales growth is strongly and inversely correlated with the presence of females among the owners. For example, a 1 percentage point increase in the share of female owners in the firm is associated with a decrease in the sales growth rate of 0.19 percentage points. In other words, moving from a firm with no female owners to all female owners is expected to be associated with decrease in the sales growth rate of 19 percentage points, a large change, given that the mean of sales growth in the sample equals only 13.8 percent. This gender-based difference in sales growth survives even after controlling for initial firm size. This finding is consistent with findings of research undertaken in other countries.[13] Similarly, firm efficiency, defined as annual sales per worker during the last year, shows a significant negative correlation with the percentage of the firm owned by women.[14]

In summary, businesses with higher female ownership tend to have proportionately more female employees in the workforce, to be smaller in size, and to be less productive. What explains the difference? Relative to male-headed firms, female-headed firms are characterized by less access to "formal" finance, are less experienced as managers, and are generally less well educated or trained.[15] But the fact that these businesses are further from the productivity frontier than their male-owned equivalents is actually an argument for prioritizing support to them, insofar as higher returns can be anticipated from a "unit" equivalent of finance or training. This is because (a) essentially the same production functions exist whether the firm is male- or female headed, given the relatively unsophisticated state of most of the enterprise sector in Somaliland; (b) the female-owned business, based on the survey results, operates with less financial and human capital input. Marginal returns on investments in female-owned firms are, *ceteris paribus*, higher. Moreover, these firms, relative to their male-owned counterparts, offer a proportionally greater number of jobs to women who are especially disadvantaged in terms of labor market participation.

Incentivizing Business Formalization

The vast majority of businesses operate informally with only an operating license or occupancy permit issued by the local municipal government. The government's perspective on formalization is that it presents an opportunity to foster greater growth and employment creation; enables the government to achieve a wide range of social benefits, including in the health, safety, fire, pension, labor, and environmental areas; and contributes to the tax base and revenues needed for the operation of critical government services. On the business side, the overall stakeholders' perspective as revealed in interviews and discussions was that the cost and burdens associated with registering formally outweigh the benefits. *Changing this cost-benefit ratio for businesses requires a re-calibration of regulatory reform that makes possible more cost efficient formalization (that is, minimizing time and cost) and links this improved formalization process with better access to new services that can enhance firm performance and the return to investor and managerial effort.*

As indicated earlier, SomPREP II seeks to address these formalization "incentive" challenges by a combined effort comprising consolidating and streamlining the registration process via the establishment of one-stop shops (OSS) and through access to the funding made available to businesses through the SBF. For these incentives to be fully effective and sustainable and provide the encouragement for businesses to invest more and contribute to the aforementioned social benefits, these incentives need to be broadly and uniformly accessible. This goes beyond the capacity of SomPREP II or any successor donor project operating as a single stand-alone intervention. But, as will be seen in the following chapters, actions can be taken by the government in the near term that would represent the establishment of the platform required for the government to more effectively leverage donor support for greater private sector and job creation outcomes.

Berbera Port Development

The Somaliland domestic market is relatively small. It is also highly dependent on regional and international trade, particularly in terms of imported consumer and intermediate goods, as revealed by the ES. As shown in figure 3.4, 85 percent

Figure 3.4 Use of Imported Inputs Is High in Somaliland

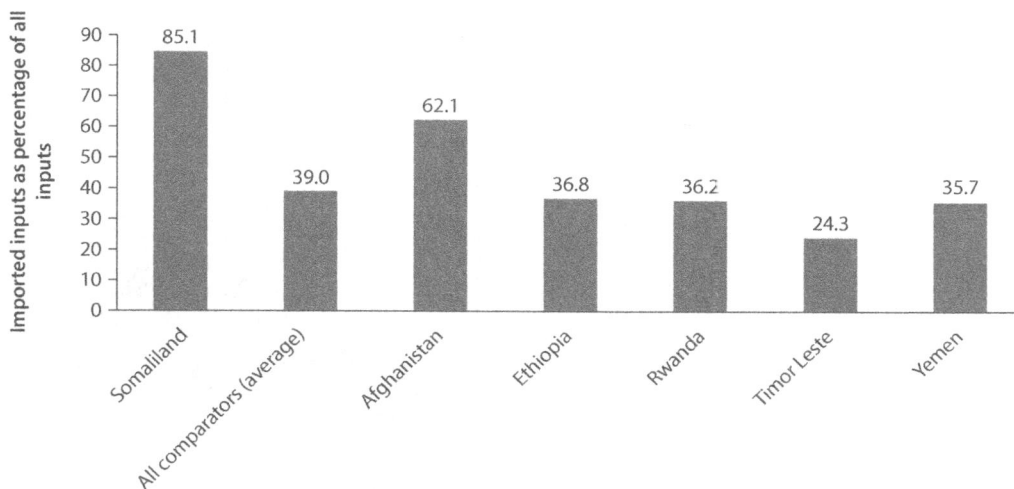

Source: Enterprise Surveys.

of all inputs used by firms are sourced from outside Somaliland. The only comparator that is close is Afghanistan at 62.1 percent. The average for all comparators is only 39 percent.

Hence, trade services—in the form of port facilities and equally important custom services (which many businesses complained were inefficient and unpredictable and not transparent in terms of the tariffs applied)—are hugely significant to the overall performance of the private sector. This is an economy which has a strategic location and is one of the port destinations—including also (primarily) Djibouti and then Somalia (Mogadishu), Kenya (Mombasa and potentially Lamu), and Eritrea (Massawa/Assab) competing for the huge entrepot trade of land-locked Ethiopia. Based on conservative projections about the Ethiopian economy, recent assessment work conducted by the World Bank (Maritime Transport and Business Solutions 2012) (see figure 3.5) indicates that the total volumes at stake amount to some 3 million TEUs (twenty-foot equivalent unit container) by 2030 in total import and export flows. General cargo import volumes via Djibouti are currently estimated to be a further 20 million tons of trade in 2013. Servicing some portion of the Ethiopian trade is a huge potential revenue source for the GoS. Revenues from ports are paid in international currencies, so it also provides an income stream that the government can use to attract foreign investment to upgrade the port facilities and capacities and hinterland infrastructure to meet this prospective demand.

For Berbera Port to be competitive in capturing some of this market and associated investment, action is required over the short term to ensure that the port itself is a well-governed, modern-run utility and the ancillary foundation services, particularly customs, are in place. These actions are important not just in them-

Figure 3.5 Djibouti Container Volume from Ethiopia

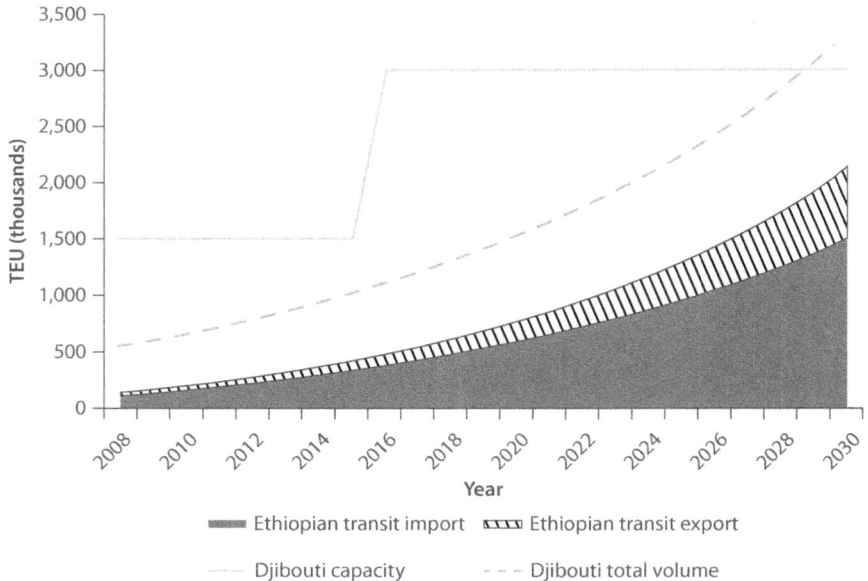

Source: World Bank Maritime Transport Business Solutions 2013 Strategic Economic Assessment of Berbera Port.
Note: TEU = twenty-foot equivalent (container).

selves but also for the signal they send as to how the GoS intends to do business with regional partner countries and international business. It also requires that the government itself further develops its capacity to effectively negotiate high-value trade arrangements with neighboring countries and potentially long-term, competitively bid public-private partnership (PPP) contracts with international companies.

In addition to the revenue windfall that a strategically developed Berbera Port can attract, it will also offer new market opportunities for innovative businesses and new forms of direct and indirect employment opportunities in multiple trade and retail services areas.

Policy Priorities for the Enterprise Sector

A diversified economy requires a dynamic private sector. This in turn will depend on the ease of entry, growth, and exit of enterprises seeking out new market opportunities. Entrepreneurialism is a key ingredient that requires a supportive investment climate. This investment climate needs to ensure that incentives to take risks in the economy are in place. Regulation needs to be balanced with promotion. And regulation needs to be efficient. Current efforts to establish one-stop shops in major city hubs in Somaliland are a first step. By making the process transparent, predictable, and streamlined, the downside of regulation is mitigated.

But this is rarely sufficient, especially in an economy so recently moving beyond a postconflict condition. It is critical that in the cost-benefit calculus of entrepreneurs, they see some net advantage to formalization. This can only come with more ready and lower-cost access to the services needed for firms to be competitive and succeed. This includes access to key factor market services (finance, infrastructure, land, labor, and skills)

To grow the enterprise sector, the following, drawn from both the conclusions of this report and the earlier *Doing Business* recommendations,[16] is required over the short and longer term.

Over the Short Term

- Acceleration of the establishment of OSS and simplification of business registration procedures throughout Somaliland to facilitate greater levels of formalization.
- Augmentation of promotional services including, over a continuing transition period towards a more inclusive financial system, an expansion in the scope of enterprise support services for the provision of key firm inputs such as seed capital, technical and vocational training, and other business services that address the current market needs and link these services—with the support of a proactive, government-led communications strategy—to firm formalization.
- Focused initiatives on those sectors and businesses with the highest probability of faster job creation growth including (a) service sectors with track record of innovation, (b) female-headed firms, and (c) start-ups in higher potential sectors.
- Establishment of a business observatory with an active and broadly representative and credible public–private dialogue structure to consult on policy, monitor and assess market development trends—including prices, industry turnover, employment levels, and competition (prices, market concentration, and conduct)—and establish the databases required to enable evidence-based assessments to be conducted. This will be critical to the credibility of the entity.

Over the Medium to Longer Term

- Follow-up on the outstanding recommendations of the *Doing Business* study.
- Introduction of a modern company law that provides clear and modern registration procedures and addresses corporate governance requirements for businesses to operate in Somaliland and mitigates the current practices of many firms to incorporate offshore.
- Introduction of an investment law that, while potentially allowing for certain fiscal and other incentives to invest, provides for other key services to enable investors to more efficiently navigate the specific risks and uncertainties that come with operating in Somaliland, including access to land and infrastructure

services, potentially via the establishment of enterprise zones or industrial parks.
- Development of the Berbera Port corridor, including—on a priority basis—the modernization of customs and clearance systems and procedures.
- Development of a master plan for land development complemented by the establishment of more effective interministerial and intergovernmental cooperation arrangements on the development of land for key commercial, industrial, residential, and public purposes.
- Improved government implementation of regulatory services—particularly related to business start-up, land acquisition and transfer, customs and trade, and licensing.

Notes

1. Under the assumption that changes in wage rates are roughly the same across firms between 2010 and 2012 or that such changes are uncorrelated with the potential covariates considered, growth rate in payroll can be used as a reasonably good proxy measure of job creation at the firm level. However, due caution is necessary in interpreting payroll as a proxy for job creation.
2. Diaspora provide up to 35 percent of start-up capital for small- and medium-sized enterprises (Hammond et al. 2011), and annual remittances are estimated to make up between 35 and 70 percent of Somaliland's GDP.
3. This difference in the financing pattern of formal and HBBs is broadly consistent with other findings in the data. For example, relative to formal firms, 29 percent of the HBBs compared with only 1.4 percent of the formal firms applied for a loan during 2012; 49 percent of the HBBs compared with 33 percent of the formal firms currently have an outstanding loan; among the firms that applied for a loan during 2012, the acceptance rate among HBBs was as high as 91.7 percent compared with 45.8 percent for formal firms.
4. Dinkelman (2011) finds that employment of females increases by over 30 percent following electrification in rural parts of South Africa.
5. An excellent review of the relevant literature on each of these issues is available here: http://wbro.oxfordjournals.org/content/24/2/233.full.
6. The Observatory of Conflict and Violence Prevention (2014).
7. This information was gleaned from interviews undertaken in context of the technical note prepared in land and real estate allocation and transfer.
8. The Observatory of Conflict and Violence Prevention (2014, 18).
9. Female-owned firms report that an inadequately skilled workforce is a major or severe obstacle more often than male-owned firms (30 percent vs. 11 percent).
10. The survey data did not allow us to identify managers by gender; however, most firms are either sole proprietorships or partnerships, so it is safe to assume that most of the managers are the owners themselves. Managers in male-owned firms are nearly twice as likely to have completed secondary school (42 percent) as managers in female-owned businesses (24 percent).

11. More in-depth analysis of the types of product/market and process innovations will be necessary to better tailor initiatives to support these activities.

12. While 64 percent of the manufacturing firms introduced a new product or service during the last year, this is not significantly different (at the 10 percent level or less) than the corresponding figure of 49 percent for the retail firms cited above.

13. A number of studies show that female-run or female-owned firms are smaller in size and also less efficient than male-run or male-owned firms. The evidence is largely restricted to developed countries. For example, Robb and Wolken (2002) analyze small formal businesses in the United States and find that female-owned businesses generate only 78 percent of the profits generated by male-owned businesses. Similar results are reported by Sabarwal and Terrell (2008) for firms in the formal sector in 26 transition countries. They attribute the bulk of this gender gap in efficiency to the relatively small size of female-owned firms. Focusing on firm size, Brush et al. (2006) among others find that in the United States, average revenue of female-owned formal firms equaled US$151,130, about 26 percent of the level for male-owned businesses. In another study on female versus male Chief Executive Officers (CEOs) based on Execucomp data, Kolev (2012) finds that female CEOs underperform their male counterparts in terms of shareholders' returns by roughly 0.35 percent per month. The gender gap in performance of female-owned businesses has also been shown to be caused by a number of factors such as the concentration of women entrepreneurs in low-performing sectors, credit constraints, cost-driven factors (less start-up capital, less business experience, less human capital) and preference-driven factors (lower self-confidence and greater fear of failure) (World Bank, Supporting Growth-Oriented Women Entrepreneurs: A Review of the Evidence and Key Challenges , 2014).

14. There is some difference in the results for sectors and firm size when using the percentage of firm that is owned by women as the measure of female ownership rather than the gender of the largest owner.

15. Female-owned businesses in the ES tend to look significantly more like the HBBs from the household survey in a number of ways: They are less likely to own land; they report more problems with theft; they are less likely to have access to electricity; they are more likely to do business with suppliers and clients that are acquaintances; and they are less likely to have paid for business development services.

16. See table 2.1 in this report for a summary of the *Doing Business* recommendations.

CHAPTER 4

Financial Inclusion and Product Diversification

The Financial Sector in Somaliland

The private sector remains constrained by a multitude of blockages which inhibit the market competition and the potential for growth that could foster investment, reduce costs, and improve quality and availability of basic products and services. A key service sector is that of finance, where access is the highest ranked constraint faced by businesses. The ES data on Somaliland (see table 4.1) indicate that 48.8 percent of firms surveyed cited access to finance as the most serious obstacle to doing business compared to a world-wide average of 16.9 percent. Moreover, if data combining "major" and "severe" obstacles are combined,

Table 4.1 Percentage of Firms Identifying Access to Finance as a Major Constraint by Economy

Economy	Year	Access to finance
World		**16.9**
Somaliland	**2012**	**48.8**
East Asia and Pacific		17.5
Eastern Europe and Central Asia		15.2
High-income OECD		11.1
Latin America and Caribbean		15.0
Middle East and North Africa		4.8
South Asia		15.7
Sub-Saharan Africa		20.5
Afghanistan	2008	16.8
Ethiopia	2011	33.2
Rwanda	2011	22.7
Timor-Leste	2009	12.1
Yemen, Rep.	2010	5.0

Source: Enterprise Surveys.
Note: OECD = Organisation for Economic Co-operation and Development.

62 percent of firms report that they are most impacted by poor access to finance.[1] This is significantly higher than the world average (32 percent), the average found in Sub-Saharan Africa (45 percent), and the average in Middle Eastern countries (41 percent). Only 1.4 percent of Somaliland firms applied for a loan or line of credit in 2012, and only 6.5 percent of firms reported no need for a loan. In the past year, approval rates for loan applications submitted in Somaliland (43 percent) appear to be about half that found in surrounding countries.[2]

Underlying these survey results is a financial sector in its infancy, lacking essential fundamentals in terms of the necessary legal, policy, and regulatory building blocks to enable greater financial inclusion and intermediation. Given these limited foundations, it is unsurprising that there is a lack of diversification in both number and type of financial service providers, as well as in products and services offered. The GoS has highlighted financial sector development—in particular the development and implementation of an effective legislative framework to regulate the financial services sector—as a policy priority to augment the provision of financial services to the economy. The SNDP identifies the weaknesses of the Bank of Somaliland (BoS) and the "absence of financial institutions—commercial and investment banks, insurance companies…" (SNDP, 76) as key challenges to be addressed. The SNDP goes on to identify the enactment of the BoS law and introduction of commercial banking laws as priority policy actions during 2012–16.

"Financial inclusion," defined as the proportion of individuals and firms that use financial services, plays a critical role in achieving shared prosperity and poverty reduction (World Bank 2014). The flagship *World Bank Global Financial Development Report* of 2014 provides evidence that the poor benefit enormously from basic payments, savings, and insurance services. In the case of small and new firms, access to finance is associated with innovation, job creation, and growth (World Bank 2014, 3). As noted above and further emphasized in the flagship report, financial services are often constrained by regulatory impediments and malfunctioning markets that prevent people and firms from accessing financial services (World Bank 2014, 3). But the challenges facing Somaliland extend further.

Unlike the surrounding countries, the financial sector in Somaliland remains largely informal and unregulated. This reality has effects on both the supply and demand for loans. Informality has implications on balance sheet structure, particularly the liability side of informal financial institutions. Informality will constrain public savings/fund mobilization and consequently available loanable funds. It is also possible that, in view of the transactional nature of available public liabilities in existing financial institutions (remittance companies), existing loanable funds remain *transitory* in nature and may not qualify as "savings" for lending purposes. Informality then becomes a key source of the inherent difference highlighted between Somaliland and comparator countries as detailed above. The very funding base for financial intermediation is undermined by the weak legal and regulatory environment. This in turn further constrains financial product diversification and the capacity of Somaliland to augment and spread the benefits of financial inclusion.

The starting point for understanding Somaliland's financial sector is the remittance industry, which transfers in excess of 50 percent of Somaliland's GNP by many estimates. The remittance institutions that have evolved have played a critical role in Somaliland's resurgence since 1991 and have afforded a measure of economic resilience in the face of the wider region's continuing insecurity.

Remittances

Large remittance inflows to Somaliland help families pay for food, education, and health services. They support small and medium-sized enterprise (SME) development, also connecting entrepreneurs in Somaliland with business partners from among the diaspora. Remittances also have major macroeconomic implications, financing imports and underpinning the local money supply.

Estimated Volume and Impact: Although the GoS estimates that some 150,000–200,000 Somaliland-born migrants are living abroad,[3] this figure could be substantially underestimated. It is difficult to determine a precise figure because other data collection sources on migrants do not count those from Somaliland separately from Somali migrants. Official statistics estimate that the Somali diaspora amounts to an estimated 1.9 million people living in the Republic of Yemen, Western Europe, North America, and other parts of the Horn of Africa in 2013,[4] with Kenya, Ethiopia, and Yemen believed to be the primary destination countries. If Somaliland accounts for about 40 percent of Somalia's total population of 10 million and contributes to a similar proportion of the overall Somali migrant stock noted above, then the Somaliland diaspora could be closer to 600,000–800,000.

In the absence of statistics on remittance flows from the balance of payments, there are no official data on the volume of remittances received in Somaliland. However remittance estimates range from US$500–$900 million per year, equivalent to 35–70 percent of GDP.[5] This makes Somaliland one of the most remittance-dependent economies in the world. The bulk of remittances come from the United Kingdom, followed by the United States.[6] A survey undertaken in Somaliland in 2012 indicates that over 40 percent of households in Somaliland receive remittances, averaging US$271 per month, or US$3,252 per year.[7] According to the same survey, remittances can represent as much as 80 percent of household income for some families and account for more than 40 percent of household income for about two-thirds of survey respondents.

These funds are a veritable lifeline. As most households receive remittances from only one migrant abroad, the degree of dependency heightens vulnerability. The extent of the remittance role in the economy is further summarized in terms of the following micro and macro factors:

- At the *microeconomic level*, the remittance inflow is felt through numerous channels. In addition to the contribution remittances make to household consumption, ES reports that most SMEs have a diaspora investment partner or received remittances to help start the company, making remittances a key source of SME finance. More specifically, while 45.4 percent of all "managers" received remittances from abroad during 2013, a greater share of those running smaller and larger firms (52.5 percent and 60.3 percent, respectively) received funds as compared to managers of micro firms (36.3 percent). Figure 4.1 illustrates the point. This suggests that those firms able to receive remittances are better able to expand business. The other consideration is that owners/managers who are relatively well-to-do (running small or large firms vs. micro firms) are the ones able to send family members abroad and benefit by way of remittances.

- The *macroeconomic impacts* of remittances are similarly significant. The influx of remittances is essential to maintaining the money supply (the "dual currency system" effectively in operation in Somaliland means availability of remittance money—mainly US dollars and Somaliland Shillings—determine liquidity). Remittances also finance imports. In the absence of a functioning national payments system, remittances routed through clearing houses in Dubai, Djibouti, or Addis Ababa are critical to settling trade payments. Money transfer operators (MTOs) are effectively the only established players in the financial sector in Somaliland, although one financial institution has obtained a license to operate an Islamic Bank and others have applied. As a result, some MTOs engage in banking activities (namely, taking deposits and making loans). The larger MTOs are using the "float" of remittances to make

Figure 4.1 In Somaliland, a Substantial Number of Business Owners and Managers or Someone in Their Household Receive Remittances

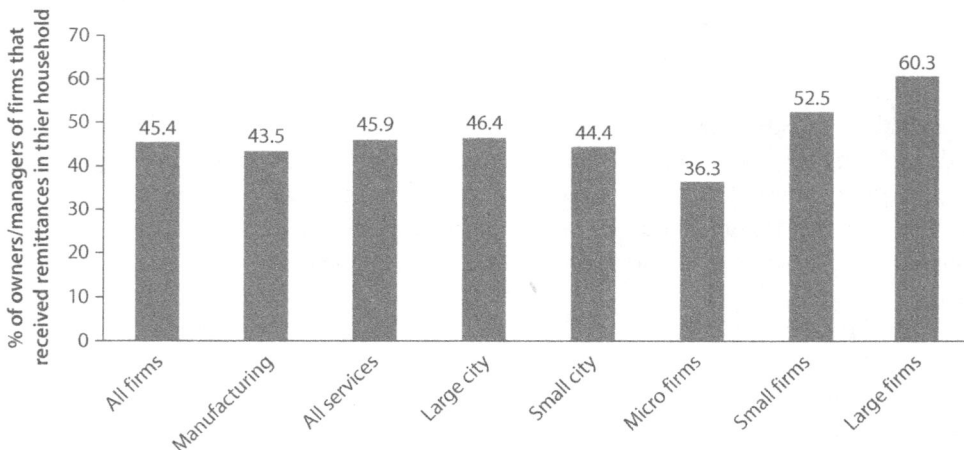

Source: Enterprise Survey.

loans and invest in the economy. Finally, remittances are essential to sustaining domestic demand and employment. With more than 40 percent of households reporting that they receive remittances, some 50 percent of consumption expenditure is made possible by remittances, much of it to purchase the essential goods not produced domestically. The MTOs are also a major source of direct, formal employment.

Remittance flow process: Transfers from the diaspora tend to be small and regular. The most common transaction size is about US$100, but the average remittance amount depends on the sending country; average transfers from the United Kingdom could be as little as Great Britain Pounds (GBP) 25 per person compared to US$170 for those originating in the United States.[8] Reported costs for making remittances to Somaliland are generally 5 percent of the amount sent up to US$1,000.[9] This is well below the total average cost of transferring funds along corridors to Africa, which was reported at 11.7 percent to send about US$200 in the first quarter of 2014, according to Remittance Prices Worldwide (RPW—a World Bank database that tracks the cost of sending money along 226 corridors, globally).[10] It is also below the global average cost of sending remittances, which was 8.4 percent over the same period.

To get a direct sense of the costs and processes of sending money to Somaliland, two remittance payments from different outlets in London, United Kingdom (see table 4.2) were initiated. The results confirmed that the price of transferring money to Somaliland is relatively inexpensive—about 5 percent.

Transaction process: The overwhelming majority of remittance transfers are facilitated through specialized Somali MTOs established in the late 1990s and

Table 4.2 Sending Money from London to Hargeisa

Sending side: London	Receiving side: Hargeisa
Location: MTO Agent (Internet café)	**Location:** MTO Branch
Total paid: £20.06	**CDD:** * Recipient was required to present picture ID, as well as the transaction code to collect funds.
Exchange rate US$/UKP: 1.6225 **Amount due to recipient:** US$32.55	**Amount collected:** US$32.00
CDD: * Sender was asked for his name (picture ID was required and copied). Address, name, and telephone number of the recipient were requested.	**FX Transparency:** Exchange rates were not posted at the branch.
Location: MTO Branch **Total paid:** £21.00 **Commission:** US$1.60 (5%)	**Location:** MTO Branch **Amount received:** US$32.00
Exchange rate US$/UKP: 1.62 **Amount due to recipient:** US$32.40	**CDD:** * Recipient was able to collect funds without showing ID once she proved to be in possession of the phone to which the money was sent.
CDD: * Sender required to present passport copy (which was scanned and oriented out) and proof of address in the United Kingdom. Details about the recipient were requested (full name, father's full name, grandfather's full name, and mobile number).	**FX Transparency:** Exchange rates were not posted at the branch.

*CDD = customer due diligence; MTO = money transfer operators; UKP = United Kingdom Pound, that is, procedures to verify and document customer identity.

Figure 4.2 Making a Remittance to Somaliland

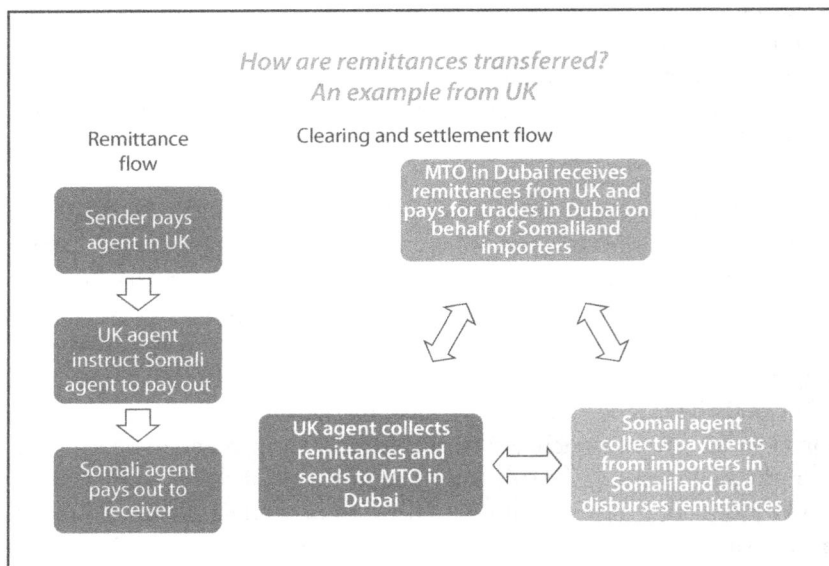

Note: MTO = Money Transfer Operator; UK = United Kingdom.

early 2000s and managed out of Dubai and Hargeisa.[11] These entities operate clearing systems in Dubai, and the United Arab Emirates (UAE), which serve as the gateway for trade finance transactions that support the clearing and settlement of remittance flows to Somaliland (figure 4.2) (Beechwood International 2013). Roughly 20 different providers offer remittance services.[12] Together, the MTOs have approximately 300 payout locations in Somaliland, as well as agents in all major cities in countries populated by Somali migrants and refugees.

Payment systems:[13] A National Payment System (NPS) infrastructure (payment clearing and settlement system) is not in place in Somaliland. The BoS does not yet have plans to build such a system or provide the services or infrastructure needed to enable financial institutions to communicate through a messaging and routing platform to transmit and reconcile payment orders, establish final positions, and settle accounts (by the debiting and crediting of accounts) among financial institutions. The integrity of any NPS relies on proper accounting for each transaction, thus stability depends on the reliability and accuracy of the clearing and settlement systems. An interbank system for communication, clearing, and settlements is needed in each country to support an efficient financial sector and to enable links to the global financial system.

In the absence of a NPS, financial institutions currently offering payment services in Somaliland operate as closed-loop systems, where each entity operates its own payment system without being interconnected to others. When financial institutions in a market are not linked through such a central platform, they are not able to process payments efficiently among each other. As a result, all payments must be processed in cash, which is extremely inefficient, resource intensive, and much more risky. Given that an interconnected system is absent in Somaliland, remittance service providers (RSPs) are not connected to any entity through which transfers into Somaliland can be directly executed. Generally, RSPs rely on commercial banks to periodically clear and settle their transactions internationally. In a typical scheme, the MTO collecting remittances in the send-ing country makes a bulk transfer to a bank, which would transfer the funds to a counterpart in the receiving country. The absence of any direct cross-border link between the local and international correspondent financial institutions abroad makes it necessary for MTOs in Somaliland to find alternative methods to clear and settle these transactions. As a result, these MTOs are forced to rely on trade-related transactions to transfer remittances into Somaliland and to meet their liquidity demands. This process is portrayed in Figure 4.2.

Another consequence of this routing scheme is that neither foreign financial institutions that send remittance payments to Somaliland nor anyone inside of Somaliland can mitigate the risks that such funds are not being used in connec-tion with illegal activities. The lack of financial supervision and regulation in Somaliland prevents foreign financial institutions from meeting obligations of their home jurisdiction that require financial institutions with which they do business to: (a) implement internal AML/CFT control systems; (b) be effectively supervised and regulated by a responsible authority for compliance with AML/CFT laws and regulations; and (c) be subject to measures that effectively miti-gate AML/CTF risks in their own institution. International AML/CFT obligations[14] call upon countries to apply effective and proportionate countermeasures against countries that do not apply these requirements, includ-ing limiting business relationships or financial transactions with such territories.[15] As a result, the scheme currently used by MTOs to transfer money to Somaliland is jeopardizing the sustainability of the financial lifeline and money transfer industry in Somaliland. Foreign financial institutions—faced with potential AML/CFT risks they cannot reasonably mitigate—are then subject to possible fines and penalties by their respective supervisory authorities.

The supervisory and regulatory environment: While remittances have been essential to the development achieved to date and will remain critical in the coming years, Somaliland's continued and heavy dependence on them is insuf-ficient to serve the financial needs of a growing and modernizing economy. Moreover, the current system of remittance transfer has limitations that poten-tially pose threats that, if not effectively addressed, may result in further isolation of Somaliland from the global financial system. In particular, this concerns the lack of prudential supervision and of systems to mitigate risks related to money laundering and other financial system abuses that can be associated with remit-tance flows. This in turn poses a potential contagion factor to foreign financial institutions that can result in a limiting and/or severing of financial relations.[16] As a result, policy makers and authorities need to build and implement systems to ensure that MTOs and other emerging financial institutions are subject to more effective regulation, oversight, and compliance monitoring. Additionally, the MTO sector as well as the broader financial sector should be subject to adequate risk mitigation systems. This includes those mandated by international (AML/CFT) requirements applicable to all countries if sustainable links to the global financial system are to be maintained.

Financial Products

Remittance companies in Somaliland also provide other basic facilities that would normally be provided by banks, including the provision of savings and current accounts to individuals, private companies, and international organizations. Many also offer trade finance and international payment services for imports through issuance of letters of credit. Other financial services are increasingly available to the private sector, principally in the form of "*murabaha*" and "*musharaka*" Islamic financing products,[17] the main modes used for financing export/import/domestic products and longer-term investment financing, respectively. The growth in financing through these vehicles appears to be robust, in particular for *murabaha*. In the case of one of the leading remittance companies,[18] *murabaha* financing grew from approximately US$500,000 in 2011 to US$6 million in 2013, and it is anticipated that this will grow still further. Increased advertising of the services and opening of new branches are thought to be some of the main drivers in increasing services to this largely underserved market demand.

The principal items being financed are building supplies and trading goods. Repayment of *murabaha* financing is currently over an average of 18–24 months. The availability of *musharaka* financing is more constrained. Financial institutions tend to require three years of financial records from a potential client in the application process. In 2013, in the case of the remittance company interviewed, *musharaka* amounted to only 5 percent of the *murabaha* financing (that is, circa US$300,000). The total client base for this remittance company was approximately 500 businesses, of which about 80 percent were Hargeisa based.

The most recent innovation is the advent of the mobile payment services (Zaad), introduced by the telecom company Telesom (see Pénicaud and McGrath 2010). This system allows customers to spend money credits loaded onto cell phones, which are accepted by a large group of merchants, from restaurants and hotels to petrol stations and universities. This service is transforming a previously entirely cash-based society in Somaliland. International providers are enabling cashless transfers by connecting to this domestic system via a global provider of wholesale carrier services in a third-party country—this allows people outside of the region to remit money directly from their electronic payment account to the "m-wallet" in Somaliland. This mobile payment service is therefore also somewhat more than just a payment vehicle. It enables Somalilanders to transfer value from cell phone to cell phone and thus serves as a stored value mechanism. However, no part of the telecommunications sector is regulated by a designated authority, including the e-money business, which presents financial risks that need to be managed by appropriate authorities.

While services are being extended to unmet market demand, there is an absence of product diversity and price competitiveness. To a significant extent this can be attributed to the limited legislation currently in place and the vagueness of some aspects of the legislation in force. As a result, what is and is not legally permissible in Somaliland is unclear and this in turn pushes up prices and reduces the appetite of financial institutions to expand services. In addition to the passage of the Islamic Banking Act, a draft conventional banking bill has been pending in Parliament for six years. Although it has gained significant support in some circles, it has not been adopted. What prevents the law from progressing (or being completely withdrawn from consideration) is not entirely clear, although it is understood from consultations with the key stakeholders that there are religious and constitutional concerns.[19] Responsible steps toward resolving this and related issues in an open and informed manner are required. In its simplest form, there are three basic policy and strategic options:

1. Prohibiting conventional financial products and services completely.
2. Limiting the use of conventional financial products and services to a specified degree.
3. Allowing Islamic and conventional financial systems to coexist.

Establishing a sustainable financial sector based on principles of inclusiveness, integrity and technical capacity will require a concerted effort by policy makers and the key policy stakeholders. This should include an objective assessment of the implications of each of the above options for Somaliland's economic development.[20] This would require, inter alia, much clearer legal foundations, definitions and operational guidelines than those existing in the current legal framework. Additionally, a thorough study should be undertaken of how the above options are implemented in other Islamic economies, the results realized, lessons learned, and likely implications for their application in Somaliland.

Currently, the Islamic Republic of Iran is the only country that absolutely prohibits conventional banking products and services. Both Pakistan and Sudan previously attempted to limit their banking systems to Sharia principles, but have since chosen to allow dual (Sharia-compliant and conventional banking) systems to exist side by side (although Sudan may revert back since the independence of South Sudan). If a more conservative approach is preferred, consideration might be given to allowing a limited number of conventional banking products and services in accordance with specified terms and conditions, with a view toward assessing results and impacts objectively and on the basis of real data within an identified timeline. The eventual decision taken by the GoS in this matter is significant in terms of the choices left to citizens and firms as to how they use and benefit from the financial sector. It is a decision that will directly impact a set of factors including price, availability, quality, reliability, and convenience. The more varied the range of effectively supervised products on the market, the greater choice and potential to realize financial inclusiveness.

The *World Bank Global Financial Development Report* (2014) states that *"Sharia-compliant financial products and instruments can play a significant role in enhancing financial inclusion among Muslim populations"* (World Bank 2014, box 1.4, 36). The report also recognizes that increasing financial inclusion through Sharia-compliant products and services requires legally well-grounded innovative approaches and practices on the part of the financial authorities and institutions to effectively address certain obstacles that can otherwise impede the financial sector capacity to sustainably and reliably meet market needs (World Bank 2014, p. 38). This includes the following:

- Lack of transparency and absence of a broadly accepted standardized process for assessing the compliance of financial institutions and products with Sharia requirements.
- Lack of information and training among public and financial experts on Islamic finance, even in Islamic countries.
- In their infancy and smaller in scale, Islamic financial products tend to be more expensive than conventional counterparts, reducing their attractiveness to consumers.

Sharia-compliant financial products and services have the potential to enhance financial inclusion, but effectively addressing the above obstacles will better ensure that individuals are able to distinguish between compliant and noncompliant institutions and products and make informed choices. A lack of certainty, and information underlying financial products and services—for instance, regarding their legality—will suppress supply and drive up prices. Aforementioned NPS and legal and institutional instruments to promote financial transparency and product diversification, such as secured transactions, credit bureaus and registries, and dispute resolutions arrangements are all absent from the financial sector in Somaliland. There appear to be no official policies or legal instruments in place to address the risks that the lack of these components create. Moreover there is currently no clear political momentum in support of their introduction or to measures needed to ensure Sharia compliance. A continuation of the currently limited financial sector will inhibit the provision of competitively priced product and service diversity.

The current lack of impetus to resolve the issue of whether or to what extent conventional financial products may exist and\or whether to focus on the development of a strictly Islamic financial system undermines the capacity of Somaliland financial sector to play its essential role in the economy. It also does harm to the perception of government capacity to effectively lead and manage important policy discussions.

The Current Legal and Regulatory Environment

A closer look at the current legal and regulatory environment for financial services reinforces the urgency to reach a decision on whether Somaliland pursues an Islamic or dual financial system development path. As noted above, the current operating environment of the remittance industry carries risks that have major knock-on effects on the functioning of the financial sector and its capacity to provide services in the wider public interest. Policy makers together with a wider set of stakeholders will need to design strategies to mitigate these risks and vulnerabilities, including strengthening regulation and supervision of the financial sector and meeting international AML/CFT obligations.

In terms of financial sector legal frameworks, the BoS Act[21] was enacted in 2012, an Islamic Banking Law[22] was adopted in 2012, and in 2013, the BoS adopted internal "Guidelines for the Licensing of Banks and Financial Institutions."[23] In addition, the government is preparing an AML bill that is anticipated to be finalized and submitted for Parliamentary approval in advance of the next election, currently scheduled for 2017. The following highlights some of the critical outstanding issues to be addressed:

- The BoS law provides the legal basis for establishment and operation of the BoS as supervisor and regulator of the financial system, but implementation is lacking due to resource and capacity challenges. The law provides for establishment of a board, as well as some general prohibitions on conflicts of interest applicable only to board members,[24] but lacks provisions setting forth ethical and professional standards applicable to the entire BoS staff, as well as clear delegation of responsibility for implementing, monitoring, and enforcing compliance. Implementation of these standards are vital to ensure the BoS can earn sufficient trust and respect from the local and international financial community to establish itself as an effective professional supervisory authority.
- The Islamic Banking Law of Somaliland, as written, presents interpretation challenges. The degree of imprecision in a number of the critical legal provisions impede effective implementation and make it difficult for officials, whatever their professional capacities, to enforce. This will, in turn, increase the potential for unpredictable regulatory supervision and the appearance of arbitrary and inconsistent decision making.

No other legal instruments exist on which effective financial supervision and regulation can be developed, and no existing laws contain the necessary provisions required by international obligations to prevent or detect money laundering and related financial crime, until potentially the draft AML bill is passed into law. Such a high degree of uncertainty in the legal and regulatory environment has compromised the ability of domestic financial institutions to maintain reliable links to foreign financial institutions and to assess and mitigate risks to make rational business and financial decisions. Further, the degree to which the BoS can earn the trust of the public, market participants (both domestic and foreign) and foreign supervisory institutions will likely be a critical factor in decisions by foreign financial institutions to establish or maintain financial ties with those operating in Somaliland. The lack of an effective and reputable regulatory and supervisory system—one that requires financial institutions to adhere to principles of safety and soundness and mitigate risks—in turn creates exposures and risks on the correspondent side. This has been a key determinant in decisions of foreign financial institutions to exit financial links with those doing business in Somaliland. If BoS credibility issues are not remedied in the near future, it is likely that authorities in more countries may pressure financial institutions under their supervision to limit or sever ties with businesses and financial institutions operating in Somaliland.

Designing and implementing the necessary financial governance, supervisory, and regulatory systems in Somaliland must also factor into consideration the realities of security and the associated risks and vulnerabilities currently prevailing in the Horn of Africa. This is critical because weaker governance arrangements, especially insufficiently supervised and regulated financial sectors can tend to attract illegal behavior and interests that seek to perpetuate the unregulated and unsupervised environments they need to thrive. Although these activities cannot be wholly eliminated by financial regulation and supervision alone, to the extent sustainable financial links to the global financial system are desired, the BoS will need to significantly improve its legal framework for supervision and regulation—including the passage and implementation of an AML law that largely meets international obligations—to ensure that the clientele the financial system serves are conducting well-supervised activities.

Beyond the limitations of the current legal and regulatory environment, the capacity to implement is also highly curtailed. The BoS has few viable internal systems or procedures that enable it to fulfill its regulatory and supervisory functions and demonstrate supervision to be "rule-of-law" based, clear, and effectively implemented and enforced, even for the legislation that is currently in place. Given the risk environment, it is even more urgent that the BoS have effective inspection systems to monitor and enforce compliance. To this end, the BoS will need to chart some clear policy objectives with a measurable implementation plan that leads to the building of an effective supervisory capacity. In this context, there is also a premium on the establishment of effective licensing systems for financial institutions already operating in Somaliland. Licensing is the crucial gateway to market entry that enables the supervisor to control participation in the market. An effective licensing process is a powerful tool to prevent and mitigate financial abuse, not only at a local level but also for cross-border flows and in the global financial system. It also provides the framework within which to develop targeted capacity-building programs.

Decisions to grant (or deny) financial licenses are among the most important decisions a financial supervisor makes, because this step is the most fundamental "quality-at-entry" control of the financial institutions that will ultimately make up the financial sector. It requires a thorough understanding by supervisory officials of all systems, procedures, policies, and an applicant's financial condition, which requires extensive documentation and analysis, as well as extensive communications between the applicant and authority. This is because prior to granting a financial license, a supervisory authority should confirm by documenting its findings that an applicant's goals and operations will contribute to the overall financial sector strategy, that the bank's financial condition is sound and does not pose any threats to the current financial system, and that it will and can operate in full compliance with all applicable legal and regulatory obligations. In addition to independently verifying and documenting the identity of beneficial owners of the applicant entity and all of its affiliated entities, the supervisory authority should confirm and document its findings that the applicant institution has adequate and effective systems and controls in the areas outlined in table 4.3.

The BoS has taken some important initial steps to establish a registration system for RSPs/MTOs and to adopt licensing guidelines for banks. But much work is still needed to reach a basic level of effectiveness to ensure that ties to the global financial community will be sustainable. For instance, the BoS should ensure that there is a clear and published regulation or fee schedule. A licensing system that aims to create a level regulatory playing field for all financial market entrants to serve a wider array of participants needs to be based on clear regulations that are also published, applied equally to all applicants, and include appeal procedures through which applicants can effectively and, on the basis of clear legal principles, challenge perceived inappropriate or adverse regulatory decisions. The new licensing guidelines approved by the BoS Board, effective September 8, 2013, show efforts on the ground to address a number of these concerns. The challenge in this instance is the strengthening of in-house governance structures and human capital at BoS that would, in turn, augment capacity to implement existing rules.

In Somaliland, progressing beyond the prevailing levels of financial inclusion and access to finance will necessitate significant improvements in the regulatory and prudential levels achieved to date. The World Bank Global Financial Development Report (2014) advises that governments focus policy actions on addressing the market failures and other dysfunctions that cause financial services to be prohibitively costly or unavailable (World Bank 2014, 3). These

Table 4.3 Bank Supervisory Checklist

Corporate governance	Credit risk	Risk management	AML/CFT
Capital adequacy	Interest rate risk	Concentration risk and exposure limits	Internal control and audit
Operational risk	Market risk	Problem assets, provisions, and reserves	Transactions with related parties
Liquidity risk	Country and transfer risks	Financial reporting and external audit	Disclosure and transparency

Note: AML/CFT = anti-money laundering/combatting the financing of terrorism.

include poorly designed and implemented legal and regulatory frameworks, poor enforcement, and inadequate competition. Information disclosure obligations on financial institutions that would enable consumers to make informed choices about risks and selection of financial institutions, products, and services, as well as seeking redress, also merit further improvement. The good news for Somaliland is that the improvement and implementation of a more adequate legal and regulatory supervisory framework has all the potential to significantly improve financial inclusion. And with a more robust enabling environment in place, there will be increased appetite to support financial institutions to extend their market operations.

Policy Priorities for the Financial Sector

The challenges facing Somaliland in building an effective financial sector remain significant. However the authorities can benefit from extensively known best practice to build a diversified, inclusive, credible financial sector that supports a level playing field for market participants and protects consumers from abuse. This system can be tailored to comply with well-defined Islamic principles. The BoS should take the lead in working with appropriate other authorities to do the following:

- On a priority basis, initiate and implement *legal and policy actions*, including (a) a broad-based informed public policy consultation involving recognized Sharia jurists to clarify important provisions in the Islamic Banking Law and the pros and cons of commercial banking; (b) passage of the AML-CFT bill to prevent criminal abuse of the financial system and bolster remittance channels; (c) implementation of licensing and registration systems, including screening processes that identify all beneficial owners,[25] assessment of internal governance systems, and effective "fit and proper" operational capacity; and (d) establishment of internal integrity systems and professional standards for BoS to become a credible supervisory and regulatory authority of the financial sector.

- At the outset, establish a *time-bound "Roadmap of Actions"* required to put in place the necessary laws, regulations, systems, and procedures identified to be currently lacking, assign accountable officials responsible for roadmap implementation, and establish an associated capacity building strategy and program to support the BoS to undertake all supervisory and regulatory functions needed.

- Over a time-bound, short- to medium-term period, work to adopt a *legal framework and NPS* so that principles of security, accountability, and inclusiveness can be achieved:
  - **Security:** Financial flows both into and out of the territory can be subject to adequate systems for documentation and traceability. This will enable financial institutions (both domestic and foreign) to meet their AML/CFT

obligations, and will provide the necessary infrastructure that will allow financial institutions to clear and settle payments through means other than manual cash transactions.

- **Accountability:** Financial product and service provision can expand in a predictable and cost-efficient manner consistent with transparent, well-defined, and "supervisable" legislative and regulatory provisions.
- **Inclusiveness:** Strengthen competition in the financial marketplace among market participants, including measures to: (i) limit the use of exclusivity agreements in the MTO sector; (ii) reduce the costs of owning accounts for the most basic financial services; and (iii) foster financial product diversification and deepening through the legally provisioned development of, inter alia, Islamic products, secured transactions and collateral registries, and credit bureaus.

- In the medium to longer term:
  - Extend *support services (for example, technical assistance, matching grants) to licensed financial institutions* to assist these entities to develop and mitigate risks of certain types of financing, including noncollateral-based lending and equity and investment instruments that can extend financial access to businesses.
  - Improve *consumer protection* in financial dealings. The lack of consumer protection further creates unnecessarily high risks for those who need financial services, particularly the vulnerable. Adopting and implementing some basic consumer protection and financial disclosure obligations, as well as designating an authority that can implement and support enforcement of these, will reduce some of the risks Somaliland citizens and companies face in leveraging their existing resources.

Notes

1. Over 62 percent of firms identify access to finance as a "major" or "severe" obstacle to running their business.
2. 85 percent in Ethiopia and Rwanda.
3. Somaliland Ministry of National Planning and Development (2011).
4. United Nations Population Division (2013). Other estimates of Somali migrants range from 1 million (Sheikh and Healy 2009, 3) to 1.5 million (Hassan and Chalmers 2008).
5. Hammond (2013, 1) estimates remittances to Somalia, based on data gathered in Somaliland and Puntland, to be a minimum of US$1.2 billion per year. Orozco and Yansura (2013, 4) estimate flows to be US$1.3 billion per year, and International Finance Corporation (IFC) data cited by the World Bank (2013, 29) put the value at US$2 billion. Cockayne and Shetret (2012, 16) estimate the flows to be US$2.4 billion a year. In the absence of official statistics for Somaliland, estimates are extrapolated from wider approximations. GDP was estimated at US$1.391 billion in 2012.

6. Information provided by Somali MTOs to Beechwood International (2013, 22).

7. In June and July 2012, 718 urban and rural households in Somaliland and Puntland were surveyed. Commissioned by the Food Security and Nutrition Analysis Unit (FSNAU), a multidonor project managed by Food and Agriculture Organization (FAO), the study examines the impact of remittance funds received by Somali households and the extent to which households share resources (both remittances and other income). Findings were published in June 2013 in a report entitled "Family Ties: Remittances and Livelihoods Support in Puntland and Somaliland."

8. Shire in Maimbo (2006, 25) reports 2004 data from Dahabshiil on mode (US$100), median (US$132.5) and average values for 90 percent of transactions (US$174.5) from the United Kingdom to Somalia. Dean, Thompson and Keatinge (2013, 69) cite data from Somali Money Services Assocation (SOMSA) for U.K. transaction size and from American Refugee Community (2012) for U.S. transaction size estimates. Interviews with MTOs with offices in Hargeisa also confirm this finding.

9. Orozco and Yansura (2013, 14). In person meetings with MTOs in Hargeisa confirmed this finding. Some MTOs also mentioned that they periodically go below 5 percent, and as low as 3 percent, during special promotion periods.

10. http://remittanceprices.worldbank.org.

11. Hassan and Chalmers (2008, 21) survey remitters in the United Kingdom, 92 percent of whom indicate that they use Somali remittance companies to send money home. This finding is confirmed by Hammond (2013, 15), who surveys recipients, and finds that 93 percent of recipients receive their money through Somali remittance companies. Hassan and Chalmers (2008, 21) find that, when possible, 21 percent of respondents also use "cash in hand" method of taking money home when travelling to Somalia, or send cash with friends.

12. According to a 2012 list of remittance companies that are registered with the BoS, this includes Oomaar money transfer, Mustaqbal express, Amaano express, Qaran express, Salaama financial, Telesom Zaad, Kaah express, Iftin express, Hodan global express, Africa express, Ladan express, Global exchange and money transfer, union for exchange and money transfer, Tawakal express, Bakal express, Amal express, Speed money transfer, Salvo remittance and exchange, Horn money transfer, Shirkada al najax. There is also Dahabshiil, while now registered as an Islamic Bank in Somaliland, also maintains a major MTO business.

13. Based on: "Review of the Market for Remittances in Somaliland on the Basis of the CPSS-World Bank General Principles for International Remittance Services," April 2014.

14. Recommendation 19, *International Standards on Combating Money Laundering and the Financing of Terrorism & Proliferation*, Financial Action Task Force, February 2012.

15. Interpretive Note to Recommendation 19, *International Standards on Combating Money Laundering and the Financing of Terrorism & Proliferation*, Financial Action Task Force, February 2012.

16. As appears to have been the case, for instance, in the recent decision of Barclay's Bank to terminate correspondent Bank services with one of the leading Somalia remittance companies.

17. *Murabaha* is a purchase and resale contract whereby banks buy goods and resell them to clients with an agreed upon mark-up. The total cost is usually paid in instalments, and this is the common system for financing purchase of physical goods. It resembles

hire purchases in that the financer pays for the good in cash and sells it to the customer in instalments. The difference between the two prices constitutes the financer's return to his capital and the risk associated with failure to repay. *Musharaka* is a partnership contract whereby the bank and the client contribute jointly to finance a venture. Profits and losses are shared strictly in relation to the respective capital contributions. This type of finance is usually employed to finance longer-term investment projects.

18. This information was obtained from interviews that took place in Hargeisa in 2014.

19. Article 5(2) of the Constitution of Somaliland states: "The laws of the nation shall be grounded on and shall not be contrary to Islamic Sharia."

20. The Tehran Times International Daily, Vol. 11672, 17 March 2013 reported that although Islamic finance assets reached more than US$1 trillion by the end of 2012, this amounted to only 1 percent of total global banking assets.

21. No. 130 (April 22, 2012).

22. Law No. 55/2012.

23. September 8, 2013.

24. BoS Law, Article 14.

25. This means the physical persons, who truly own or control decision making and manage assets of the legal entity or legal arrangements.

CHAPTER 5

The Government Regulatory and Promotional Role

The Government Sector in Somaliland

In any economy, the government is a critical provider of services to business. At a minimum, it needs to provide macroeconomic stability, policy development, infrastructure (where it cannot be provided through private investment), and a legal framework, with secure contracts, property rights, supportive regulations for enterprises and banking, and an ability to enforce those regulations. In a postconflict economy or in a developing economy where there is a particular need to stimulate investment and growth, there is also a premium on a proactive promotional role in the provision of fiscal, financial, and nonfinancial support. As has already been seen in the case of financial inclusion, the challenges to government legislative, policy, and implementation capacity are substantial and greater when set in a context of fragility with political, technical, and financial resource constraints such as those faced by the GoS. Selectivity and sequencing will therefore play a central role if an optimal path of regulatory and promotional capacity development is to be achieved. A first step in mapping out the role and needs of the GoS in private sector engagement is to provide an assessment of the capacity of government institutions to support private business. That is, to assess the arrangements in place, GoS has to (a) regulate and (b) promote PSD activities and identify key areas for institutional change and capacity building as economic recovery and development proceeds.

The small size and relatively low capacity of the present government administration is largely a product of the civil conflict that started in 1991 with the collapse of the Somalia state that had existed under the Siad Barre government. This resulted in a destruction of infrastructure, a significant decline in private business activities and tax revenue and a lack of government authority and effective regulation. This was in contrast to the period during the 1970s and 1980s when there was intrusive state control of the productive sector through direct ownership of production capacity and heavy regulation. Over the past 20 years, the government's regulatory authority has slowly recovered, but its promotional role is, as yet, hardly developed.

In addition to the legacy of the civil war, an understanding of the subsequent evolution of the government sector since this time must also take into account ethnic and clan dynamics. The level of clan homogeneity of the government service affects its functional capacity in a number of contradictory ways. For example, homogeneity tends to strengthen coordination and decision making in the administration, while diversity may create tension and dysfunction. Furthermore, diversity can bring with it a risk of inefficient operation through the excessive proliferation of government ministries and agencies and unclear division of labor.[1] On the other hand, diversity, if it is well managed, may increase the credibility of governmental authority across Somaliland and the respect for central decisions. The final consideration is that private business has relied on traditional measures based on trust to regulate business, such as in the enforcement of contracts. Trust is in turn bound up with clan and subclan membership.

The SNDP makes the following statement:

> The limited capacity of public institutions is a major obstacle that stands in the way of implementing the national development plan and the realization of Vision 2030. The national capacity in terms of the effectiveness of institutions, and the quality of human resources available is low and must be addressed strategically. The strategy must aim at building the capacity of central government institutions, local governments, private sector enterprises and community organisations. There have been many capacity building projects supported by international organizations over the years. Unfortunately, these have been fragmented, ineffective and often non-aligned with national development priorities.

One aspect of the civil conflict has been Somaliland's very small government revenue base. As recently as 2012, it was still only about 5 percent of GDP approximately US$80–100 million. This is significantly lower than the Sub-Saharan Africa average and also that of other conflict states. On the other hand, external aid exceeded US$100 million in 2012. This is still a relatively small percent of GDP but very high in relation to total government expenditure by international standards. Despite its relative youth, external aid to Somaliland is also already very fragmented, and much of it is off-budget. Fragmentation and lack of coordination of development projects create additional difficulties for the establishment of a government structure in line with national planning objectives.[2] Leaving aside the emerging effects of aid fragmentation, there remains a relatively clean slate for the development of governmental institutions because of the lack of a recent history of state control and relatively weak vested interests in maintaining control. The restricted budget and size of government does provide an opportunity to focus attention on prioritizing essential government roles in the economy and "right-sizing" government support to, and regulation of, the private sector.

The SNDP reported serious weaknesses in civil service staffing. Thirteen percent of staff were over retirement age or absent from their posts, and 17 percent of a sample of staff (in the Ministries of Planning, Finance, Justice, Aviation and Labor) failed a test of competency and were put on training programs provided by the Civil Service Institute (CSI). Following these findings, a presidential decree of December 2010 instructed the Civil Service Commission (CSC) and the Civil Service Reform Ministerial Steering Committee (CSR MC)[3] to implement civil service reforms adopted by the Cabinet. Currently, aspects of the reforms are under way.

The GoS embarked upon a major effort to strengthen the civil service by bringing in new staff, with numbers increased by 30 percent from 2010 to 2011, and a further significant expansion over 2011 to 2013. The Ministry of Finance nearly doubled its total staff between 2012 and 2013, especially in the professional/ managerial grade, where numbers tripled with the hiring of a batch of university graduates, mostly in accounting, economics, and information technology (IT), largely to boost the tax and customs inspectorate. A similar increase took place at the Ministry of Justice, where the number of legal professionals tripled between 2011 and 2014. The ministries responsible for agriculture and industry doubled their staff over 2009 to 2013, again with emphasis at the professional level. Other ministries, such as the Ministry of Fisheries, have reported similar increases, and the Ministry of Posts and Telecommunications increased its staff by over 50 percent. While increases in the civil service professional or paraprofessional complement are essential to the conduct of government in Somaliland, the new hires are largely inexperienced in the particular sector to which they have been allocated, and a major capacity building exercise is needed going forward.

The Bank's 2013 Public Expenditure Review (PER) also reported on a number of key weaknesses. It noted that informality of decision making together with *ad hoc* changes in the structure of ministries were leading to uncertainty in government operations and budgeting. Confusion between government ministries in relation to their scope of responsibilities has also been exacerbated by informal change in ministry mandates. A need for better coordination among ministries has been brought into focus particularly because of the establishment of new ministries spinning off from "parents" (such as the Industry and Water ministries, which have taken over roles previously managed by the ministries of Commerce/Industry and Mineral Resources/Energy). This has created additional funding challenges. For instance, the Ministry of Industry, newly formed in 2012 with an important role in private sector development, has yet to receive substantive resources.

The PER recommended a multidimensional approach to the development of the governmental system to: (a) promote certainty in government structures setting clear mandates for each ministry and avoiding the excessive creation of new ministries and Special Commissions and; (b) implement civil service reform, including retirement of overage civil servants and reduction of costs. What follows, in support of these broader government sector recommendations, is an effort to assess the supply and demand conditions for government services to the private sector.

The Business Demand for Government Services

The demand for government services from the private sector is the starting point for structuring the government's engagement with business. To find out what regulatory and promotional functions are most lacking, the major obstacles to business were reviewed at the sector and enterprise levels. A number of sources of information were tapped to identify these, including the SNDP, the ES and *Doing Business* report, the USAID Business Confidence Index, and the Somaliland Investors Guide.[4]

First, under the SNDP the main constraints on private business were reported to be inadequate infrastructure, high cost of fuel and electricity, lack of access to credit and financial sector facilities, inability to obtain international insurance or guarantees, time-consuming procedure for setting up companies, taxation on wealth or capital for start-up businesses, limited technical skills, and absence of business support institutions. The key approaches by the GoS to meet these challenges as set out in the SNDP are as follows:

- Create a legislative framework to regulate the financial services sector.
- Reform business laws.
- Establish PPP modalities.
- Develop a private sector development policy.
- Carry out a private sector needs assessment.
- Strengthen the capacity of business associations and chambers of commerce.
- Create a conducive, business-friendly investment climate.
- Establish a business management information system to develop e-commerce.
- Rehabilitate and build infrastructure: roads and power generation and lines.

Second, modifying the findings of the SNDP (which, for example, did not list land issues), the Bank's ES[5] found that Somaliland businesses faced a relatively narrow range of particularly severe problems, especially in lack of access to finance and inadequate land rights and titling, which together comprised 74 percent of the overall perceived obstacles to business, far higher than the average for Sub-Saharan Africa. Transport, tax rates, and electricity were the other significant factors, amounting to a further 20 percent.

As detailed in the earlier chapters, policy challenges for the government are wide ranging. Credit has been constrained by the failure to adopt a sufficient and comprehensive set of banking laws and up to now, based on the information available, has only been accessible for key clients of remittance companies. Land has been a severe obstacle because of conflict-related disputes over land title and the inadequacy of the land registry. The Urban Land Management Law covers land disputes, but there is confusion over which government agencies, central or local, have jurisdiction over sales or allocation of land, and the status of private landholding in general. The burden of tax rates found by the ES was similar to that elsewhere in Sub-Saharan Africa. In the case of infrastructure, evidence from the ES indicates access to power to be a lesser problem and access to transport services a greater problem than is the case for the rest of Sub-Saharan Africa.

To take into account the obstacles to business in Somaliland represented in all the available sources (*Doing Business*, ESs, the Business Confidence Index, and the SNDP), the results were combined.[6] This was done on an indicative basis since the rating of the severity of the obstacles was not always either quantified or comparable. A matrix of key problems and their severity are shown in table 5.1.

The aggregate scores approximately confirm the order of obstacles found in the ES—with access to finance as the top constraint and land access issues in second place. The SNDP ranking, representing the perceptions of the GoS, diverge more sharply, with poor infrastructure seen as the major obstacle to business.

Table 5.1 Average Survey Rating as Obstacle to Business

Source of data	Enterprise survey	Doing business indicators	Business Confidence Index/ investors Guide	SNDP	Average rating H=3, M=2, L=1
Access to finance and insurance	High	High	High	Medium	**2.75**
Access to land (registration, title)	High	Medium	High	n.a.[a]	**2.66**
Access to electricity	Medium	Medium	High	High	**2.5**
Start-up costs: licensing/registration	a/[b]	High	n.a.	Medium	**2.5**
Legal enforcement (judiciary)	n.a.	High	Medium	n.a.	**2.5**
Infrastructure (roads)	Medium	n.a.	Medium	High	**2.33**
Tax payment	Medium	High	Medium	Medium	**2.25**
Skilled labor	Low	n.a.	Medium	Medium	**1.66**
Lack of business support institutions	n.a.	n.a.	n.a.	Medium	n.a.

Source: World Bank enterprise survey, 2012 Doing Business in Hargeisa Report, USAID business confidence index, Somaliland National Development Plan.
Note: The "high, medium, and low" categories are subjective based on the information provided in the various reports. n.a. = not applicable.
a. Areas which are n/a are deducted from the denominator, which may bias results.
b. a/: The ES covered registration and licensing of enterprises and obtaining of permits, but these did not figure significantly in barriers to entry and so were not included in the overall final analysis.

The Supply of Government Services

The key government agencies: Having focused up to now on the demand side of the market for government services, this section now considers the supply side. For this purpose, a self-assessment survey was conducted of 16 ministries to assess the perceived capacity, responsibilities, competence, and skill needs of government ministries dealing with private business.[7] The survey results were complemented by ministry strategy and plan documents. Based on the principal constraints to business identified in the last section, six of the government ministries/agencies are key to private business development, as shown in table 5.2.

Analysis of government's responsibility to regulate private business: The government agency functional responsibilities for the *regulation* of private business may be divided into five main categories: (a) development of policy and legal framework; (b) policy supervision and enforcement; (c) licensing and registration; (d) monitoring and inspection; and (e) taxes and levies. The self-assessments revealed the following ratings of capacity in the five regulatory areas (table 5.3).

Bearing in mind the possible biases of self-assessment, the ratings for all responding agencies show overall capacity for regulation at just below the midpoint of 5.0. Finance, Energy, Water, and Justice show themselves at above the midpoint, while the six other ministries and the municipality that have reported are below the midpoint. Overall capacity is therefore just less than acceptable according to the self-assessment criteria used here, with considerable scope for upgrading. Within the six key agencies (referenced with the letter 'a', the table does not include the Bank of Somaliland), average self-assessment was regarded as acceptable (5.37), but there is clearly scope for improvement.

Within functions, capacity in licensing and registration for all agencies shown is generally regarded as acceptable, with an average score of 5.9. The next highest score is for taxes and levies, where the overall score is also above the midpoint of the range. Policy development capacity is at the midpoint. These areas are

Table 5.2 Obstacles to Business Growth and Main Agency Responsible

Obstacle to business by level of severity	Responsible government agency
Access to finance (via banks and nonbank institutions)	Bank of Somaliland
Access to (public) finance and taxation issues	Ministry of Finance
Land issues, urban services (zoning, markets, roads, electricity); business licensing and promotion	Municipal/District Agencies
Electricity and other energy sources	Ministry of Energy
Business start-up/licensing and business development services	Ministry of Commerce and Investment
Judiciary, commercial disputes, legal enforcement	Ministry of Justice
Vocational training and skills development	Ministry of Labor

Table 5.3 Self-assessment Scores for Capacity in Key Regulatory Areas

Ministry/local government	Policy/legal framework	Policy supervision/ enforcement	Licensing/ registration	Monitoring, inspection	Taxes, levies	Average score
Ministry of Commerce and Investment[a]	3.00	2.00	9.00	1.00	6.00	4.20
Ministry of Finance[a]	8.00	5.00	n.a.	4.00	5.00	5.50
Ministry of Justice[a]	7.00	7.00	5.00	n/a	n/a	6.33
Municipality of Hargeisa[a]	4.00	4.00	5.00	5.00	6.00	4.80
Ministry of Labor[a]	4.00	3.00	6.00	6.00	4.00	4.60
Ministry of Industry	3.00	2.00	7.00	4.00	5.00	4.20
Ministry of Agriculture	4.00	4.00	5.00	5.00	5.00	4.60
Ministry of Fisheries	5.00	3.00	5.00	3.00	n/a	4.00
Ministry of Energy[a]	6.00	8.00	7.00	6.00	7.00	6.80
Ministry of Water	8.00	4.00	4.00	8.00	4.00	5.60
Ministry Post and Telecoms	3.00	3.00	6.00	2.00	6.00	4.00
Average Score	5.00	4.09	5.90	4.40	5.33	4.94

Note: n.a. = not applicable.
a. identifies a "key" agency in terms of role dealing with priority private sector constraints.

relatively well understood and have been in place for the longest time, even though it is generally recognized that they could function much better. The weakest scores are for supervision and enforcement and for monitoring and inspection. This is most likely because these functions require more specialized skills, systems, and experience. For the seven key agencies, the pattern of capacity is similar, with especially low ratings for these two sets of functions, even though the overall average competence score was higher. Capacity building going forward would therefore need to be focused on these upstream policy supervision and downstream regulatory inspection functions, both for the seven key agencies and more generally within government.

The major problems for government can be divided into internal capacity problems of the agencies themselves and problems connected with the wider external environment. These problems are largely common to all ministries in the government, as evidenced from the survey, from all the Ministerial Functional Reviews (MFRs) so far conducted, and in the SNDP.

Internal Impediments: The most general problem across the GoS is a severe shortage of funds, which affects all functional areas. The GoS budget has increased steadily but, as stated, remains very low as a percent of GDP. More specifically, the financing constraint has led to the following:

- An urgent need for new buildings and renovation of old, civil works (for example, access roads and utility installations), equipment, and facilities (laboratories, housing, stores, appliances, telecoms).

- Shortage of professional-level staff and skills, and inadequate management and staff organization.
- Poor motivation due to inadequate salaries and pension provisions (which in turn motivate staff to work less but to stay beyond formal retirement), and lack of work organization.
- Lack of computerized management/information systems to assist management control, recordkeeping, inspection, compliance, monitoring, and reporting.
- Lack of adequate personnel manuals, job descriptions, contract arrangements, and structured career paths.
- Need for outside expertise to help upgrade staff quality and design/introduce new programs and services.

Looking at the full list of government agencies surveyed, there are certain standouts. For example, the technical departments of the Ministry of Energy and Minerals and the Ministry of Water and Health need laboratory equipment and special training in using laboratory facilities if they are to fulfill their inspection mandates. The same applies to the newly formed Quality Control Commission (not surveyed), which has to send samples outside for testing, causing unacceptable delays so that it is generally not possible to test pharmaceutical products prior to their entry into the market. The office of the Attorney General is mandated to legally incorporate certain categories of firms but does not have the lawyers to fulfill this mandate, while audit firms are not sufficient to provide the mandatory annual accounts.

In the case of the judiciary, 90 percent of sitting judges have not studied beyond secondary school, and there is a lack of commercial dispute resolution capacity and inadequate funding for commercial lawyers and legal research capability. Inspection capacity and compliance in several ministries are constrained by lack of equipment such as computers to set up centralized and efficient information systems. The Ministry of Finance only recently started to recruit adequate numbers, but has yet to place trained staff into the tax inspectorate. The newly created Ministry of Industry remains severely short of personnel. In the BoS as detailed earlier in this report, major reorganization is needed to complete its transition to a fully functioning institution. Licensing of banks is so far limited to Islamic banking, with a conventional banking bill still pending. Regulations for Islamic banking supervision are not developed, and Bank of Somaliland (BoS) supervision capacity is only now beginning to be developed, but remains hindered by lack of legal and regulatory clarity. There is a broad lack of professional staff, and only recently there has been an effort to inject a significant number of university graduates into the civil service.

External impediments: Widely cited problems connected with the external environment include the following:

- Lack of credibility of government decisions and lack of understanding of regulations, leading to low compliance.

- Incompleteness of laws and regulations (for example, lack of final gazetting) governing activity to regulate and promote private business.
- The need to simplify and clarify regulations to assist business development.
- Complexity of supervision/enforcement and inspection/monitoring functions—for example, multiple regulators dealing with business entry (to be addressed partly through the one-stop shop project).
- Failure to apply formal laws, effectively leading to utilization of traditional systems.

In the case of quality standards, the lack of general acceptance up to now of the government oversight role has resulted, for example, in many enterprises trying to avoid controls and selling expired goods. Fulfillment of ministerial responsibilities in enforcement and inspection is similarly constrained by lack of legal enforcement capacity, and the lack of external audit capacity within Somaliland, which, as stated, prevents information being sent to the company registry to conduct its business. The internal constraints of ministries expected to enforce standards (such as the Ministry of Health) in turn create an external constraint for those such as the Ministry of Justice, which cannot enforce the law if evidence of lack of compliance is not available.

Analysis of GoS's ability to promote private business: In general, the founding regulations of the ministries are relatively silent on promotion as compared with regulation. The survey thus prompted responses based on the set of government functions that are regularly carried out in other countries, divided into eight categories for the survey: (a) sector strategy/policy; development (b) fiscal instruments; (c) financial instruments; (d) nonfinancial support; (e) employment support; (f) infrastructure provision; (g) PPPs; and (h) public–private dialogue.

The survey asked for self-assessments of promotional capacity by the ministries using the same approach as for regulation functions. The ratings provided are on average significantly lower (at 3.92) than for regulatory capacity, while several ministries did not provide any information at all in this area. Interviews suggested that the relative lack of development of promotional systems was because, whereas a minimum level of regulation was essential and was also a source of government revenue, promotion generally requires a higher level of expertise within government and uses up scarce budgetary funds.

In the Ministry of Finance, tax regulations have been developed over the course of years since the start of recovery, while promotional measures such as tax and tariff incentives (for example, tax holidays and waivers) have been applied relatively unsystematically to individual industries and are in their relative infancy as a promotional tool. Enterprise financing schemes such as support to lending through credit insurance or guarantees have not been attempted. In the Ministry of Commerce and Investment the same applies: business registration and licensing practices that are income generating are in place, while assistance services such as trade and business advisory centers have not been started.[8]

The low response rate and gaps in information on promotional questions does limit the analysis. Nevertheless, with this limitation borne in mind, the overall average assessment is well below that for regulation. Of the agencies reporting, only the Ministry of Finance rates itself as having adequate capacity to promote, but it provides responses in only two areas: fiscal support and employment support, with the latter function self-rated below the mid-point. Capacity for developing promotional schemes for financing, provision of infrastructure, and the development of PPP projects is particularly weak across almost all agencies, which is in turn also a reflection of the limited financial sector capacity in Somaliland.

The survey highlights the main capacity-building problems in the promotional area to be essentially the same as those for regulation, that is, a combination of internal capacity constraints associated with funding, equipment, skills, and motivation and a set of external constraints associated with inadequate laws and regulations, inadequate compliance and enforcement, resolution of disputes. However, in the case of business promotion, the capacity gaps are greater because in a number of government departments the concept of promoting, rather than simply regulating, private business has not yet been developed. For example, the Ministry of Finance is in control of a fiscal regulatory program of taxation and is developing a public finance management capability, and it has put in place some fiscal incentives such as export tax rebates and tax and tariff holidays for start-up enterprises on which it gives itself a high rating. But public financial instruments, such as loan guarantees and export credits, which are common in other developing economies, have not yet been attempted. In the Municipality of Hargeisa, there are plans to start business promotion services and develop targeted infrastructure programs, but these initiatives are still at the idea stage.

Table 5.4 Self-assessment Scores for Capacity in Key Promotional Areas

Ministry/ Local Government	Strategy/ policy	Fiscal support	Financial support	Non-financial support	Employment support	Infra	PPP	Public Private Dialogue	Average Score
Ministry of Finance		8.00			3.00				**5.50**
Municipality of Hargeisa	6.00			0.00	7.00	5.00	5.00	4.00	**4.50**
Ministry of Labor, Soc. Welfare	4.00	2.00	1.00	3.00	4.00		2.00	3.00	**2.71**
Ministry of Industry	7.00	5.00	8.00	6.00	4.00	2.00	0.00	2.00	**4.25**
Ministry Agriculture	4.00				3.00	3.00	3.00	3.00	**3.20**
Ministry of Energy	0.00	0.00	0.00	5.00	4.00	6.00	3.00	9.00	**3.38**
Average Score	4.20	3.75	3.00	3.50	4.17	4.00	2.60	4.20	**3.92**

The promotional aspect of PPPs are inhibited not just by fiscal constraints, but also the lack of a regulatory framework which is needed to allow PPPs to go ahead effectively within the municipalities and the Ministry of Public Works. On a more positive note, there is a sense that public–private dialogue is relatively effective largely because of the proactive character of the Somaliland private sector, including the diaspora, over a long period of time.

Development of a Capacity-building Strategy

The need for capacity building to regulate and promote private business: While first steps have been taken, much remains to be done. The institution building strategy going forward will need to achieve more of a balance between the revenue-generating needs of the government and the promotional needs of private business. While regulatory functions are being developed, they remain weak and training and equipment needs are considerable, not as much in the licensing and taxation areas but particularly so in the supervision and inspection areas. The private sector promotion functions of government, whether fiscal, financial, non-financial, or in regard to broader factor market issues, such as financial sector development and employment promotion, are still further behind. Physical constraints such as rapid urban growth are also putting considerable strain on start-up government services.

Mapping of constraints and skill requirements against government capacity: The identification of a strategy for capacity building in government in the context of the special problems of a postconflict or fragile society requires prioritization of the institutions and functions to be supported going forward. This can be seen to involve a three-step process:

- **Step 1.** Mapping the major obstacles to business against the government agencies with the responsibility to address these obstacles to identify the key responsible agencies.
- **Step 2.** Mapping all surveyed government agencies against the main types of functions required in the areas of *regulation* and *promotion* of private business, to show those with the largest "span of engagement".
- **Step 3.** Identifying the main capacity-building needs in the key agencies with the widest span of engagement to effectively carry out these functions.

Step 1 resulted in the identification of the six key agencies. Step 2 provided a rating of the span of engagement with the private sector of all the agencies surveyed. Step 3 took the findings of Step 1 and Step 2 and identified their main capacity-building requirements. While it is clear that some of the individual sector ministries (such as the newly formed Ministry of Industry) urgently need capacity building, it is proposed that the most effective starting point is to focus on those ministries and agencies that are regarded by private business as performing a cross-sector function in critical areas.

Table 5.5 maps and rates all six key ministries/agencies with responsibilities for addressing the most severe business obstacles against the principal regulatory and promotional functions examined that they are, or should be, performing. This shows which of the key agencies are most engaged with private businesses across the functional areas in which they need help.

The ministries agencies which have the most engagement with private businesses are the municipalities and the Ministry of Commerce and Investment. Municipalities provide the widest range of business regulation and support services at the "ground level". This includes municipal responsibility over other agencies that deliver municipal services (for example, infrastructure such as access roads, electricity, water and waste management). The main exceptions to municipality responsibility are the provision of fiscal and financial instruments and centralized support such as for trade and foreign investment, which would continue to be the role of central government, and for which the municipalities would have to coordinate with central government agencies (such as Finance and Commerce and Investment).[9]

Table 5.5 Functional Roles of Key Ministries in Main Areas of Regulation and Promotion

Government Agency[a]	Ministry of Finance	Ministry of Justice, Courts	Ministry of Trade and Investment	Ministry of Labor and Social Affairs	Ministry of Energy	Municipal/ District Authorities
Strategy and Policy	X	X	X	X	X	X
Legal and Regulatory Development	X	X	X	X	X	X
Regulation, for example licensing and registration	n.a.	n.a.	X	X	X	X
Taxes, subsidies and incentives	X	n.a.	X	n.a.	X	X
Nonfiscal promotion measures	n.a.	n.a.	X	n.a.	X	X
Public financial instruments, funds/ guarantees	X	n.a.	n.a.	n.a.	n.a.	n.a.
Trade promotion measures	n.a.	n.a.	X	n.a.	n.a.	n.a.
Skill formation programs	n.a.	n.a.	n.a.	X	n.a.	X
Industrial infrastructure provision	n.a.	n.a.	X	n.a.	X	X
Public–private partnerships	n.a.	n.a.	n.a.	n.a.	X	X
Public–private dialogue	n.a.	n.a.	X	X	n.a.	X
Span of Responsibility	4	3	8	7	6	10

Source: World Bank survey of government institutions conducted in 2013.
a. Note that the president's office also engages with the private sector through, for example, the dialogue process.

Capacity and training needs of key agencies: Comparing the government ministries' regulatory capacity self-assessments with their importance in addressing the key obstacles facing business, the main need for capacity building is in supervision and enforcement and in monitoring and inspection. Some, notably the Ministry of Commerce and Investment also assessed themselves as weak in the policy area. The Ministry of Energy was the only ministry dealing with key obstacles to business that also rated itself 'satisfactory to strong' in supervision/enforcement. In the promotional area, the information provided suggests that there was weakness across the board, and the area where a number of government ministries felt the greatest need for capacity building was in forming PPPs.

Policy Priorities for the Government Sector

In an economy so reliant on its private sector, much still depends on the accelerated development of the government sector and its capacity to develop, introduce, and credibly implement key institutional, legislative, and regulatory arrangements. Added to this is a clear role to collaborate with the private sector to undertake promotional initiatives to address market failures that hinder private sector risk taking and investment. Recalling the priority areas set out in the earlier section on business demand for government services and those actions recommended in the chapters on the enterprise and financial sectors, table 5.6 provides a summary of key capacity building requirements in order for government to be able to address these priorities. This summary draws also both the survey results from the government ministries and other agencies and the ministries' own published plans. It represents a considerable development program.

Going forward, the insight that local government has a specially broad engagement with private business on both the regulatory and the promotional sides[10] suggests, in particular, that the government's role in private sector development in Somaliland requires not just a careful consideration of the future balance of regulatory and promotional action, but also the future balance of central and local government action. A large part of the responsibility could beneficially focus at the local government level. This especially applies to activities such as business licensing, inspections, and enforcement (for example, of industrial pollution controls), settlement of land disputes, development of commercial and industrial space and services, improvement of urban or ex-urban access roads, water, provision of business support services, participation in PPPs for infrastructure development and service delivery, and dialogue with the private business community.

Table 5.6 Main Capacity-building Needs Stated by Key Agencies Engaged with Private Sector

	Regulatory Area	Promotional Area
Ministry of Commerce and Investment	Simplify registration process Licensing technology systems Registration data management Data collection and statistics on commodities Increase number of staff at professional advisors level	Export market database Business and investment policy framework One-stop shop business entry program Foreign investment law trade strategy/policy negotiation Training in assessing potential investment areas; private business data collection system (profiling)
Ministry of Finance	Establish electronic database (DBMS) for taxes and VAT control Increase capacity in technical, administrative, and database skills Develop regulations and procedures for donor/beneficiary multiyear programs for ministry funding Introduce internal and external audit and controls	Strengthen economic policy development Develop tax incentives for the private investments with growth and employment opportunities Develop expertise in incentives for priority inputs such as agricultural materials and fertilizers Develop further expertise in areas of tax incentives, and public funding mechanisms for business including guarantees and credit insurance. Strengthen public procurement process
BoS	Major training program for about 100 professionals in BoS functions affecting private sector, including macroeconomic research, bank supervision, procurement, and risk management	Training and advisory assistance in commercial banking sector policy development, regulation, bank analysis monitoring and supervision, reorganization, payments systems, banking operations, licensing and registration Training in supervision of nonbank financial institutions —capital market, foreign exchange dealers, payment service, payment system, and securities service providers
Ministry of Justice	Training of professional staff for justice sector monitoring and reporting. Establishment of legal training and resource center for judges and court administrators Establish combined district, regional and appeals courts; Attorney General, legal aid, office of Ministry of Justice in each region. Complete major enabling legislation on judicial independence and code of conduct, and capacity to dispose of commercial disputes Expand court staff; land dispute resolution; legislative drafting unit in the office of the Attorney General; real property registry in Regional Court of Appeals; Bar Association; professional law librarians	

table continues next page

Table 5.6 Main Capacity-building Needs Stated by Key Agencies Engaged with Private Sector *(continued)*

	Regulatory Area	Promotional Area
Municipality	Training in management of broad area of regulation and service provision GIS-based tax system for building licenses Stabilization of tax revenue base	Building capacity in strategic planning and urban planning Building links with the private sector to develop PPP projects in the municipality Strengthening project management capabilities in service provision including infrastructure development (for example, market places, access roads, bus network, maintenance services) Strengthening capacity to manage dialogue with private business
Ministry of Labor and Social Affairs	Increase capability in inspection of work places Improve capacity for recording and resolving of trade disputes, delivering judgments Strengthen facilities for issuance of work permits to create a favorable environment for labor movement into Somaliland	Increase cooperation with Ministry of Finance to provide tax exemptions to attract diaspora Increase capability to formulate programs for self-employment and entrepreneurship development Increase capacity for employment funds, pension schemes, job creation, including credit and grant schemes. Develop job centers to facilitate exchange of labor market information; increase advocacy of employment rights and employment advisory capacity, especially for youth Improve capacity to cooperate with Ministry of Education on vocational training system and to develop placement programs and internship programs for youth.
Ministry of Energy	Legal and regulatory development in power and mining Improve capacity of information and data banks, transport and logistics for service delivery Enhance training of ministry professionals and skilled technicians in regulatory area, including exposure visits to international energy institutions Enhance training for drafting energy regulations Enhance expertise in mining law, codes, and licenses	Develop expertise in design and implementation of PPPs in the energy sector

In the short to medium run, adequate capacity does not yet exist in the municipalities to carry such a burden of broad business regulation and support programs. So for now, the initiative for new support programs will need to be taken at the central level. The main exception is in the critical area of land use, where there will need to be a demarcation of responsibility between the Ministry of Public Works, other central ministries, and the municipalities. However, in the longer term, the way ahead may be for the government to delegate significant responsibility for implementation of a broad range of small- and medium-scale business regulation and promotion measures to the municipal level.

Notes

1. For example Rural Development and Environment was split from the Ministry of Livestock (to form the Ministry of Rural Development and Environment) apparently to allow the appointment of a new minister representing a particular political faction. The Ministry of Industry and the Ministries of Water and Industry were recently split off from other ministries partly to establish clan balance.

2. The structure of government could be distorted if the pattern of external funding is inconsistent with the government's development priorities. For example, Department for International Development (DFID)'s Somalia Operational Plan, which provides funding to Somaliland, differs from the priorities set in the SNDP (PER, p. 23)since it does not include transport and water as priority areas. Danish International Development Agency (DANIDA)'s Somalia Program 2011–14 also does not specify these subsectors. Both focus more on private sector job creation, growth, and basic service delivery.

3. The Steering Committee comprises the Minister of Finance, National Development and Planning, Justice, and the Minister of Labor and Social Affairs.

4. The Somaliland Investors Guide and Business Confidence Index were developed by the Ministry of Commerce and Investment of Commerce with the help of USAID. See Ministry of Trade and Investment (2014).

5. The ES was conducted by the Bank during 2013 using a sample of 500 enterprises.

6. A focus group of enterprises offered further guidance on the key constraints, emphasizing the cost of electricity, insurance as a major constraint on foreign trade, and lack of court capacity especially for commercial disputes which have to be resolved informally at the family, subclan, and clan level.

7. The self-assessment ratings were for functions performed or expected under their respective statutory legislation, while functions which were not so required are shown as "n/a." The possible range was "0" (zero) to "10" (impossible to improve on). The ministry self-assessments were conducted with interviewer guidance to ensure as far as possible consistency across institutions. Self-assessment may provide different results from outside assessment, but it is justified in that it provides an insight into how far the government is aware of its own capacities. Any tendency for a ministry official to overestimate capability may be to some extent counteracted because a high score would tend to suggest that outside assistance would be focused elsewhere.

8. The Ministry of Commerce and Investment has however been the counterpart agency for the Bank's Somalia Private Sector Development Re-engagement Program Phase II (SomPREP II) project, including the Somaliland Business Fund (SBF), and for other projects such as the USAID grant fund.

9. Not surveyed but potentially important was the recently established Quality Control Commission, which is expected to play the role of a Bureau of Standards with oversight and regulation of private processing, manufacturing, and distribution on both the input and output sides.

10. And in other areas such as public procurement of private goods and services.

CHAPTER 6

Economic Governance and Political Economy Choices

The Evolving Challenges to Somaliland Economic Governance

For the purposes of this report, economic governance is understood in the following terms as the "structure and functioning of the legal and social institutions that support economic activity and economic transactions by protecting property rights, enforcing contracts, and taking collective action to provide physical and organizational infrastructure" (Dixit 2009, 5). Economic governance is both a major responsibility of government and the point in public policy processes where political and economic interests directly intersect. Getting economic governance right is a critical prerequisite for sustained economic development. Among other things, it requires the following:

- Passing appropriate legislation and tailoring policies to create an enabling environment for private sector growth while also protecting consumers, workers, and the state.
- Developing a tax code that is perceived as fair, that is enforced universally, and that provides the government adequate funding to operate without imposing undue burdens on firms and citizens.
- Developing sufficient governmental capacity to implement policies and regulate the economy.
- Ensuring that government is accessible, responsive, and accountable to citizens without being captured by particular interest groups.

Given its current regional status, recent history, and deep and long-standing clan-based and political culture, Somaliland has a unique set of factors at play that impact the current status and potential evolutionary path of its economic governance arrangements. These need to be understood in order to more effectively identify the challenges and opportunities to economic governance appearing on the horizon.

The limits of informal governance: Earlier in this report, the strengths of the Somaliland economy were noted and in particular the capacity of Somaliland to establish economic exchange through a trust based on social and cultural mores. But as the economy progresses and strives to meet the more complex demands of a maturing and growing population, the negotiated, informal arrangements that have served Somaliland well in earlier postwar years are increasingly shown to be insufficient for its next stage of economic growth and investment. The signs of this changing reality are revealed in the analytical work undertaken for this report. Somaliland ranks among the most difficult places to do business in the world (World Bank 2012, 1). The ESs identify a range of factors that impede or discourage private sector investment. These obstacles are further confirmed by the diaspora dialogues and the consultations that accompanied the analytical effort.

Looking more deeply at the leading constraints such as finance, land, and water, of note is the differential impact that these constraints have on different strata of the private sector. For instance, small businesses reported different experiences of investment constraints than larger businesses; female-headed firms face additional constraints to their productivity; and diaspora expressed concerns that their capacity to invest is hindered by perceived uneven treatment in some areas, such as access to land and dispute resolution. A general finding is that large enterprises are in a much stronger position to address and resolve impediments to doing business in Somaliland than are small firms and microenterprises. Large businesses can gain access to credit abroad, procure their own power, import skilled labor, and use their money and social capital to ensure land disputes are resolved in their favor. Large firms enjoy certain advantages in all economies but are arguably in an even more privileged position to benefit from the current system of negotiated arrangements with the government. Smaller firms have weaker bargaining positions with the government and complain of inconsistent and costly administration (for example, in customs), which breeds distrust of the government and animosity toward what is perceived to be the potential for collusion between large firms and the government.

In several sectors (for instance, import–export, telecommunications, and remittances), the potential exists for more powerful businesses to shape public policies in ways that can discourage or prevent new competition in those sectors. As has been portrayed in the foregoing chapters, the government currently has a limited legal, regulatory, and institutional capacity available to deal with this dynamic. This leaves the government ill-equipped to properly manage the issues and maintain its accountability to the wider population. The worst-case scenario is one where there is policy capture, which can severely reduce government legitimacy as steward of the public interest. This is not an issue easy to address in Somaliland, given the current lacuna of objective data and the ever-present concern not to diminish the track record and huge strides that have been taken— by both public and private sectors—since 1991. However, interviews and focus group feedback consistently voiced this concern. Somaliland does not want for engaged political discourse among its citizens, so it is not surprising—given the size of top private sector firms in Somaliland in contrast to the modest capacity of the government—that concerns about government autonomy on critical matters of economic governance are being raised. If these concerns are not objectively addressed with evidence and transparency, there is a risk of eroding public confidence in the otherwise impressive democratic system in Somaliland.

An imperative for institutional development: To take advantage of current and future economic opportunities, especially nonremittance external sources of investment, Somaliland must accelerate its transition to greater reliance on formal economic governance tools and uniform application of laws and policies. If not, Somaliland risks becoming trapped in economic governance arrangements that will produce a low-level equilibrium and missed opportunities, as well as declining political legitimacy. Informal, negotiated arrangements between the government and private sector actors or between private sector firms pose too many risks for investors. These arrangements work against new investors with little or no social capital in Somaliland which, in turn, is currently the primary source of the trust relations at the heart of Somaliland's current political economy.

Overall the evidence to date signals an institutional-building effort that has made progress in developing formal structures of economic governance. However, where much remains to be done within this framework. For instance, the legislature's ability to understand and address complex technical aspects of economic governance is variable. Moreover, the formal judiciary is not relied upon by most citizens and firms to adjudicate disputes or enforce contracts. At the level of the executive, there was—during the consultations and interviews— views expressed that the presidency role in decision-making needs to be put onto a more formal institutional footing. At the level of the Somaliland government— as portrayed in chapter 5— "clusters of competence" exists in a variety of offices and ministries, but generally the capacity of the civil service to implement and enforce policies is low. The effectiveness of ministries and municipalities typically depends on the quality and commitment of one or two individual leaders, so cabinet rotations can have dramatic impact on the quality of a ministry's performance. This is not a surprising finding, as political institutionalization is a slow process that can, even in best case conditions, take a generation and longer. In the absence of a sufficiently professional government institutional capacity, a government can be more easily penetrated by strong societal (clan) and private sector interests. All this in turn impacts the center–periphery dynamics and the impact of the election cycle. Some comments on each of these factors follow.

Clannism. Somaliland is a lineage-based society in which clan and subclan identity play an important role. Clan has an ambiguous role in Somaliland. On one hand, the social contract between clans has been central to maintaining peace, and clan-based customary law has been the main source of routinized dispute management. On the other hand, clannism can work against the principle of meritocracy in employment and contract distribution, encourage neo-patrimonial behavior, and is at the heart of some of the most intractable disputes over property and rights. Clannism is ubiquitous in Somaliland politics: the role of clan elders is institutionalized in the Upper House or Guurti; citizenship is based on clan; voting strategies are heavily influenced by clan calculations designed to maximize the number of seats a lineage has in Parliament; an informal understanding has been in place that the presidency rotates among major clans and subclans; the Ministry of Labor sometimes reviews hiring practices to ensure acceptable distribution of jobs along clan lines; and the ongoing tensions in eastern portions of Somaliland over affiliation with Somaliland, Puntland, or a self-declared autonomous Khatmumo region are clannish in nature.

Core-Periphery Dynamics. As with Somaliland's informal economic governance arrangements, the aspects of clannism that helped Somaliland maintain peace and stability now risk becoming an obstacle to good governance and private sector growth as Somaliland enters a new phase of development. This tension is liable to intensify if the government is unable to diversify its economy, not just in terms of greater access to opportunity in different sectors of the economy but also geographically. Economic investment and wealth are heavily concentrated in the capital Hargeisa and more broadly in the Berbera-Hargeisa-Boroma corridor. Most of the rest of Somaliland has seen limited development. Lineages that are dominant in the core area have benefited more from Somaliland's private sector investments. A concerted effort is required to mitigate the perception and evidence of privileged access and build a more inclusive private sector development paradigm.

Democracy and elections. Somaliland's multiparty democratic system is another impressive accomplishment. Election campaigns are, however, an important entry point for powerful private sector lobbying in the political arena. Parties and top political figures accept contributions from large firms which, in the absence of clear legally enforceable rules for accepting and using election contributions, leave open the perception that preferential benefits are involved. These arrangements are a source of frustration for smaller businesses.

Managing Change with Structural Transformation

The case for the status quo: Somaliland is a high-risk investment environment due in part to its unrecognized political status and the complications that this creates. The research done for this report confirms that local private sector actors have done an impressive job of both calculating and managing risk primarily through traditional mechanisms, given the limited institutional and regulatory structures built to date, albeit from a very low postconflict base. It has also led to caution towards stronger economic governance measures that create new uncertainties, by altering an operating environment in which many in the private sector have found a level of security and in which a significant number has managed to thrive.

Given this context, pursuit of more robust economic governance will need to include a focus on producing shorter-term positive impacts to reassure businesses of the long-term value of an effective regulatory environment. Nevertheless, the outstanding political economy question that bears close monitoring is whether the current informal institutional arrangements and policy-making practices of the Somaliland government are viewed as a transitional state, or as a preferred condition to satisfy the interests of those that would want to perpetuate in an operating environment of informal governance. The present evidence is mixed, suggesting that initiatives to promote new modes of more formal governance will be the source of both support and contest within civil society, the private sector, and government itself. The challenge is likely to become even more complex over the coming years as potentially transformational economic developments could significantly impact the economic and policy interests among Somaliland's key stakeholders.

Sources of change: Three economic developments in particular—hydrocarbon extraction, expansion of the seaport, and expanded transit trade with Ethiopia—have the potential to reshape the Somaliland economy, creating a significant increase in government revenues, attracting large direct foreign investments, and creating new opportunities in information and service sectors. This foreign investment is already starting to flow with the recent investments by foreign firms including Somcable, Coca-Cola, and Genel Energy. Port and transit trade expansion and the discovery of hydrocarbons could rapidly accelerate direct foreign investment, potentially bringing with it needed capital investments, technology transfer, and job creation. It will also add a powerful new dimension to the political economy equation.

The other consideration to note is that these developments have the potential to change the Somaliland economy into what is known as a "rentier" economy—one in which most government revenues accrue from the "rent" it captures from natural resources or real estate rather than from taxes on citizens. This can have the effect of shifting the commanding heights of an economy from the private to the government sector. The pathologies of rentier states are well known, often linked to the so-called resource curse, and serve as a cautionary note. In the wrong circumstances—conditions of low levels of institutionalization and accountability and low commitment to national development—rentier states can result in spikes in corruption, authoritarianism, and power struggles. When governments with strong rule of law, accountability measures, and commitment to the future are in power, windfall revenues from natural resources and seaports and DFI flows are more likely to be harnessed to promote rapid economic growth and political stability in the interests of the Somaliland people.

In addition to the new sources of economic growth now appearing on the horizon, questions can be asked about the future of the current mainstay of the economy—the remittance flow. Few diaspora in the world are as dedicated to remitting money to family members on a monthly basis as are Somalis and Somalilanders, a unique advantage that reflects the powerful obligations binding this diaspora to its extended families. But the fact that remittances constitute 40–50 percent of the Somaliland GDP is a worrisome level of dependence on an external source of funding that, while reliable, is vulnerable to disruptions due to economic downturns, changes in welfare programs in host countries, and banking regulations. It raises concerns about the long-term sustainability of the Somaliland economy. The finding that 40 percent of Somaliland households receive remittances, averaging US$271/month, and that the urban middle class remains dependent on remittances underscores that households receiving remittances form something of a privileged class in Somaliland. This system creates enormous incentives for households to focus their livelihood and investment strategies on placing a family member overseas, despite the very high cost and risks involved. Evidence from other research (for example, the *UNDP Human Development Report of 2011*) finds that the remittance-focused economy shapes educational choices as well, as young people pursue language and other skill sets mainly crafted to make them employable overseas. The heavy reliance on remittances means that Somaliland's top export is its own labor force.

As the second generation of the diaspora that commenced in earnest in the early 1990s starts to earn a living, it will be of particular significance if this new generation of Somali immigrants and refugees are less willing to remit money to family members they barely know. This suggests that the remittance economy on which Somaliland is currently based is unsustainable without a continued flow of citizens abroad. Tightening immigration laws in the West and efforts to indigenize labor in the Gulf could make this more difficult in years ahead. There is a possibility that the current generation of remittances constitutes temporary windfall revenue that will slowly decline in importance.

Whether Somaliland becomes more of a rentier than a remittance economy depends on factors like the size and extractability of oil and Somaliland's ability to stay connected with the new generation of diaspora, both of which are largely beyond its control. What it can control is its preparations for such a scenario—the pace and effectiveness of policy reform and institution building. If Somaliland engages in the difficult task of economic governance reform now, it stands a much better chance of adapting to potential changes in remittance flows and harnessing new wealth from trade and oil toward transformational growth in the economy. Though the actual changes in the economy have not yet occurred, Somaliland today is at the "pivot point" in its economic development. In sum, Somaliland is approaching a critical crossroad; the decisions its leaders take on these matters will determine the course of Somaliland for decades to come.

CHAPTER 7

Conclusion

The Political Economy at Work

Somaliland has already experienced two decades of major changes in its security situation, its political system, its economy, the regional environment, and technological changes. In the process, Somaliland and its people have demonstrated impressive resilience and capacity for progress—both politically and economically. The Somaliland of today bears very little resemblance to the Somaliland emerging from the war and dislocations of the early 1990s. Politically, Somaliland featured very significant adaptability and innovation in the 1990s, from the Boroma peace conference to the passage of the Constitution in 1999, which transitioned the government from a clan-based form of representation to a multiparty system. Somaliland also demonstrated its political adaptability with its hybrid governance model, which enshrined the role of customary authorities (clan elders) in the Upper House or Guurti. In a region with various forms of more authoritarian government, Somaliland has remained committed to a liberal democratic model.

Over the past 15 years, however, the political system can be seen to have grown less able to respond to changes in the economy, society, and wider regional setting and is having difficulty keeping up with changes in the private sector. Everywhere, political institutions and governance models tend to be slower to adapt than their counterparts in civil society and the private sector, so Somaliland is not unique in this score. Politics is driven and constrained by competing interests, compromises, and slow decision-making processes. In the case of contemporary Somaliland, the gap between the speed of potentially transformational changes in the wider political economy and the pace of the government response runs the risk of missed opportunities on a large scale.

From the political economy perspective, the analysis undertaken from this report points to the following conclusion. The principal impediment to business, as documented by the survey (including access for finance, insecure land title, costs of and access to infrastructure services) all reflect shortcomings in core economic governance. Additional concerns raised during diaspora and local business interviews that taxes and customs are opaque and unevenly applied further highlight the deficit in terms of policy focus and implementation. It is not just about the policy and legal framework but also very much about the capacity—both technically, but also politically—of government to implement in an even-handed, transparent, and predictable fashion and provide a level playing field to domestic, diaspora and international investors.

Private Sector Development and Jobs Creation—Policy Choices for the Future

Many rightly laud the more traditional coping mechanisms discussed in this report. It has provided the bedrock for much of Somaliland's success to date. But the proposition of this report is that this model of economic development is reaching a point of significantly diminishing returns and an increasing inability to meet the demands of a population that is seeking opportunity and jobs and a closer integration with the world economy. There is an opportunity and necessity to generate a step-change level of new investment flows and to access new markets to spur broad-based economic growth. But it requires that Somaliland takes the dynamic and robust culture that has served it so well through very difficult times and joins this to a drive for institutional development and internationally recognized standards of economic governance.

This renewed drive towards objectives that the GoS itself has set out as policy goals in the SNDP would provide a clearer path towards a more robust diversified economy with greater capacity to provide the jobs that Somaliland requires. And while there are larger regional political issues to be addressed by the GoS, the private sector development policy options available for pursuit at this juncture remain entirely within its purview. They can be acted upon now. This conclusion echoes recommendations from many other quarters for Somaliland to build its capacity to deliver economic governance and judicial functions through formal institutions and laws, and not via informal arrangements. This will involve a transitional period in which both formal and informal mechanisms play essential but overlapping roles. There are many risks associated with this transition, one of which is incautious policy initiatives that undermine informal mechanisms of economic governance and enforcement of contracts when they are still needed. The transition will require carefully calibrated legal and policy shifts implemented over time with careful management of the vested interests they will impact. What would be the core features of a policy agenda designed to respond to the greater international, regional, and domestic pressures that the economy will be facing in the coming years?

The following represents a summary of main priorities, as they pertain to the financial, enterprise, and government sectors that have been the focus of this report.

- **Financial Sector:** Somaliland needs to get its financial sector into better shape. It should pursue and conclude decisively on its current ongoing debate as to the nature of this sector and whether it is to be a solely Islamic financial or alternatively a dual system. Once this decision is made, move purposively to amend and introduce the necessary legislation so that an effective regulatory system can be operationalized, and this absolutely key sector can provide the inclusive services that the economy so desperately needs.
- **Enterprise Sector:** Facilitate formalization and new business entry and target services to those businesses with near-term employment and growth potential, including firms with a track record for innovation and female-headed businesses. Develop enterprise zones and industrial parks where it will be possible to mitigate infrastructure and land access risks more systematically. Ensure that these services are allocated to interested businesses in a transparent and accountable manner and in accordance with well-defined and documented eligibility criteria. The other key infrastructure investment priority is development of the Berbera Corridor. But this is not just about capital investment; it must also entail governance development and modernization of other key related services—in particular the customs administration.
- **Government Sector:** Ensure that capacity building to and investment in government and other public agencies (for example, the BoS and Berbera Port) are aligned closely with policy milestones, the passage of critical legislative instruments and regulations, and initiatives being taken for the enterprise and finance sector—as outlined above. Put in place a metrics program and align institution building and training closely to progress on these higher-level development outcomes.

Concluding Remarks

Somaliland's maintenance of peace and security is a signature accomplishment and must be safeguarded. Conflict sensitivity is required in all aspects of economic governance to ensure that goals designed to catalyze private sector growth do not undermine Somaliland's sustained peace. The World Bank's *World Development Report 2011: Conflict, Security, and Development* concluded that "strengthening legitimate institutions and governance to provide citizen security, justice, and jobs" is critical to breaking conflict cycles and maintaining peace (World Bank 2011, 2). It is significant that all three of these government deliverables are also central tasks of economic governance to promote private sector growth.

In its diagnosis of resilience and vulnerability to political violence, the report found the following:

Many countries face high unemployment, economic inequality, or pressure from organized crime networks but do not repeatedly succumb to widespread violence, and instead contain it. The WDR approach emphasizes that risk of conflict and violence in any society (national or regional) is the combination of the exposure to internal and external stresses and the strength of the "immune system," or the social capability for coping with stress embodied in legitimate institutions. Both state and non-state institutions are important. Institutions include social norms and behaviors—such as the ability of leaders to transcend sectarian and political differences and develop bargains, and of civil society to advocate for greater national and political cohesion—as well as rules, laws, and organizations. (p. 7)

Applying the World Development Report (WDR) findings to the Somaliland case is revealing. First, Somaliland currently performs well in two of the three critical tasks associated with consolidated peace—provisioning of security and justice. It falls far short on the third objective of generating employment, however. The legitimacy of its institutions is generally high, but threatened by some of the factors noted above, especially public perceptions that the government is too susceptible to private sector capture. The WDR makes the point that the societal "immune system" to political violence requires strong institutions at both the state and nonstate level. In the Somaliland case, informal institutions are currently more central than formal state structures to peace maintenance; this suggests Somaliland's "immune system" is functional but incomplete, and that Somaliland's ability to consolidate peace requires stronger governmental institutions.

Perhaps the most important aspect of the WDR is how it highlights a difficult transitional challenge in Somaliland. Strengthening of formal economic governance and capacity is needed to attract investment that will spark growth and reduce unemployment. But that needs to be done without compromising the constructive role that informal institutions have to date played in maintaining peace and providing justice. Somaliland's strategy for pursuing formal economic governance will need to ensure that informal governance arrangements are not disrupted abruptly during the long transitional period of institution building. The continuation of pluralistic legal systems for dispute mediation is one example of how formalization of economic governance can be achieved in a conflict-sensitive manner, as part of an intentional transitional strategy designed to ease disruptions while shifting from informal to more formal economic governance.

References

Aghion, Philippe, Thibault Fally, and Stefano Scarpetta. 2007. "Credit Constraints as a Barrier to the Entry and Post-Entry Growth of Firms." *Economic Policy* 22 (52): 731–79.

Aiello, Francesco, Alfonsina Iona, and Leone Leonida. 2012. "Regional Infrastructure and Firm Investment: Theory and Empirical Evidence for Italy."*Empirical Economics* 42 (3): 835–62.

American Refugee Community. 2012. "Facilitating Remittances for Humanitarian Purposes."

Aterido, R., and M. Hallward-Driemeier. 2007. "Impact of Access to Finance, Corruption and Infrastructure on Employment Growth: Does Sub-Saharan Africa Mirror Other Low-Income Regions." Policy Research Working Paper 5218, World Bank, Washington, DC.

Bank for International Settlements and the World Bank. 2007. "General Principles for International Remittance Services." Basel, Switzerland.

Beck, Thorsten, Asli Demirgüç-Kunt, Luc Laeven, and Ross Levine. 2008 "Finance, Firm Size, and Growth." *Journal of Money, Banking and Credit* 40: 1379–405.

Beck, Thorsten, Asli Demirgüç-Kunt, and Vojislav Maksimovic. 2005. "Financial and Legal Constraints to Firm Growth: Does Size Matter?" *Journal of Finance* 60 (1): 137–77.

Beechwood International. 2013. "Rapid Assessment 'Safer Corridors': Case Study on Somalia and UK Banking." Report for Her Majesty's Government, September.

Brush, C., N. Carter, E. J. Gatewood, P. Greene, and M. Hart. 2006. *Growth Oriented Women Entrepreneurs and Their Businesses* (New Horizons in Entrepreneurship). Cheltenham, UK and Northampton, MA: Edward Elgar.

Carlin, W., M. E. Schaffer, and P. Seabright. 2006. "Where are the Real Bottlenecks? A Lagrangian Approach to Identifying Constraints on Growth from Subjective Survey Data." Discussion Paper 2006/04. Centre for Economic Reform and Transformation, Edinburgh.

Claessens, Stijn, and Luc Laeven. 2003. "Financial Development, Property Rights, and Growth." *Journal of Finance* 58: 2401–36.

Cockayne, James, and Liat Shetret. 2012. "Capitalizing on Trust: Harnessing Somali Remittances for Counterterrorism, Human Rights and State Building."Center on Global Counterterrorism Cooperation.

DAI. 2011. "Partnership for Economic Growth." United States Agency for International Development (USAID), USAID East Africa/LPC Somalia, July.

Dabla-Norris, E., M. Gradstein, and G. Inchauste. 2008. "What Causes Firms to Hide Output? The Determinants of Informality." *Journal of Development Economics* 85: 1–27.

Dabla-Norris, E., and A. Feltenstein. 2005. "The Underground Economy and Its Macroeconomic Consequences." *Journal of Policy Reform* 8 (2): 153–74.

Dean, Aimen, Edwina Thompson, and Tom Keatinge. 2013. "Draining the Ocean to Catch One Type of Fish: Evaluating the Effectiveness of the Global Counter-Terrorism Financing Regime." *Perspectives on Terrorism* 7 (4): 62–78.

Demirgüç-Kunt, Asli, Inessa Love, and Vojislav Maksimovic. 2006. "Business Environment and the Incorporation Decision." *Journal of Banking and Finance* 30: 2967–93.

Dinh, Hinh T., Vincent Palmade, Vandana Chandra, and Frances Cossar. 2012. *Light Manufacturing in Africa: Targeted Policies to Enhance Private Investment and Create Jobs.* Washington, DC: World Bank. http://go.worldbank.org/.

Dinkelman, Taryn. 2011. "The Effects of Rural Electrification on Employment: New Evidence from South Africa." *American Economic Review* 101 (7): 3078–108.

Dixit, Avinash. 2009. "Governance Institutions and Economic Activity." *American Economic Review* 99 (1): 5–24.

Djankov, Simeon, Ira Lieberman, Joyita Mukherjee, and Tatiana Nenova. 2002. *Going Informal: Benefits and Costs, The Informal Economy in EU Accession Countries.*" Bulgaria: Center for theStudy of Democracy.

Dollar, D., M. Hallward-Driemeier, and T. Mengistae. 2005. "Business Climate and Firm Performance in Developing Economies." *Economic Development and Cultural Change* 54: 1–31.

Escribano, A., and J. L. Guasch. 2005. "Assessing the Impact of the Business Climate on Productivity Using Firm Level Data: Methodology and the Cases of Guatemala, Honduras, and Nicaragua." Policy Research Working Paper 3621, World Bank, Washington, DC.

Fajnzylber, P., W. F. Maloney, and G. Montes-Rojas. 2009. "Releasing Constraints to Growth or Pushing on a String? Policies and Performance of Mexican Micro-firms." *Journal of Development Studies* 45 (7): 1027–47.

———. 2011. "Does Formality Improve Micro-firm Performance? Evidence from the Brazilian SIMPLES Program." *Journal of Development Economics* 94: 262–76.

Farrell, Diana., 2004. The Hidden Dangers of the Informal Economy. http://www.mckinseyquarterly.com/.

Food Security and Nutrition Analysis Unit (FSNAU). 2013. "Family Ties: Remittances and Livelihoods Support in Puntland and Somaliland."

GDS. 2011. "Value Chain Analysis for the Gums/Resins and the Fisheries Sectors in Somaliland." Report to the World Bank.

Goldsmith, A. A. 1995. "Democracy, Property Rights and Economic Growth." *Journal of Development Studies* 32 (2): 157–74.

Gundel, Joachim. 2006. *The Predicament of the 'Oday:' The Role of Traditional Structures in Security, Rights, Law, and Development in Somalia.* Nairobi: Danish Refugee Council and Oxfam/Novib.

Hammond, Laura. 2013. "Family Ties: Remittances and Livelihoods in Puntland and Somaliland." Nairobi: Food Security and Nutrition Analysis Unit (FSNAU) Somalia.

Hammond, Laura, Mustafa Awad, Ali Ibrahim Dagane, Peter Hansen, Cindy Horst, Ken Menkhaus, and Lynette Obare. 2011. "Cash and Compassion: The Role of the Somali

Diaspora in Relief, Development and Peace-building." United Nations Development Program.

Hassan, Mohamed Aden, and Caitlin Chalmers.2008. "UK Somali Remittances Survey." Published by DfID, SendMoneyHome.org and Profile Business Intelligence Ltd.

Jaramillo, M. 2009. "Is There Demand for Formality among Informal Firms? Evidence from Micro Firms in Downtown Lima." German Development Institute Discussion Paper 12/2009, Bonn.

Kolev, G. I. 2012. "Underperformance by Female CEOs: A More Powerful Test." *Economics Letters* 117: 436–40.

La Porta, R., and A. Shleifer. 2008. "The Unofficial Economy and Economic Development." Brookings Papers on Economic Activity, Economic Studies Program, The Brookings Institution, 275–352.

LeSage, Andre. 2005. *Stateless Justice in Somalia: Formal and Informal Rule of Law.* Geneva: Centre for Humanitarian Dialogue.

Levine, Ross. 2005. "Finance and Growth: Theory and Evidence." In *Handbook of Economic Growth*, edited by Philippe Aghion and Steven N. Durlauf, 865–934. Amsterdam: Elsevier.

Lewis, I. M. 2002. *A Modern History of the Somali.* 4th ed. London: James Currey Press.

Lewis, William W. 2004. *The Power of Productivity: Wealth, Power, and the Threat to Global Stability.* Chicago: University of Chicago Press.

Lipscomb, Molly, A. Mushfiq Mobarak, and Tania Barham. 2013. "Development Effects of Electrification: Evidence from the Topographic Placement of Hydropower Plants in Brazil." *American Economic Journal: Applied Economics* 5 (2): 200–31.

Loayza, N. 1996. "The Economics of the Informal Sector: A Simple Model and Some Empirical Evidence from Latin America." *Carnegie-Rochester Conference Series on Public Policy* 45: 129–62.

Maimbo, Samuel. 2006. "Remittances and Economic Development in Somalia: An Overview." World Bank Social Development Paper no. 38, Washington DC.

Maritime Transport and Business Solutions. 2012. "Strategic Assessment of the Berbera Port." Prepared on contract to the World Bank.

McKenzie, D., and Y. S. Sakho. 2010. "Does It Pay Firms to Register for Taxes? The Impact of Formality on Firm Profitability." *Journal of Development Economics* 91: 15–24.

Ministry of National Planning and Development of Somaliland. 2011. "National Development Plan (2012–2016)."Hargeisa.

Ministry of National Planning and Development of Somaliland. 2011. "Somaliland National Vision 2030." Hargeisa.

Ministry of Commerce and Investment 2014. "An Investment Guide to Somaliland Opportunities & Conditions 2013–2014."Hargeisa.

North, D., and R. Thomas R.1973. *The Rise of the Western World.* Cambridge: Cambridge University Press.

Orozco, Manuel, and Julia Yansura. 2013. "Keeping the Lifeline Open: Remittances and Markets in Somalia." Published by Inter-American Dialogue, African Development Solutions and Oxfam America.

Pénicaud, Claire, and Fiona McGrath. 2010. "Innovative Inclusion: How Telesom ZAAD Brought Mobile Money to Somaliland." GSMA Mobile Money for the Unbanked.

Rajan, Raghuram G., and Luigi Zingales. 1998. "Financial Dependence and Growth." *American Economic Review* 88: 559–86.

Robb, A., and J. Wolken.2002. "Firm, Owner and Financing Characteristics: Differences between Male and Female-owned Small Businesses." Working Paper, Federal Reserve Board of Governors.

Rosenberg, N., and Birdszell, L. E. 1986. *How the West Grew Rich: The Economic Transformation of the Industrial World.* New York: Basic Books.

Sabarwal, Shwetlana, and Katherine Terrell.2008. "Does Gender Matter for Firm Performance? Evidence from Eastern Europe and Central Asia." IZA Discussion Paper Series No. 3758, World Bank, Washington, DC.

Sheikh, Hassan, and Sally Healy.2009. "Somalia's Missing Million: The Somali Diaspora and its Role in Development." Published by UNDP.

Straub, Stephane. 2008. "Infrastructure and Development: A Critical Appraisal of the Macro Level Literature." World Bank Policy Research Working Paper 4590, World Bank, Washington, DC.

The Observatory of Conflict and Violence Prevention. 2014. "Baseline Assessment on Land Ownership and Land Right in Somaliland." http://ocvp.org/docs/SOM_OCVP%20JCCP_BRLOLRS_February_2014.pdf.

Torstensson, J. 1994. "Property Rights and Economic Growth—An Empirical Study." Kyklos 47 (2): 231–47.

UNDP. 2011. "Human Development Report of 2011." New York.

United Nations, Department of Economic and Social Affairs. 2013. Trends in International Migrant Stock: Migrants by Destination and Origin (United Nations database, POP/DB/MIG/Stock/Rev.2013).

USAID. 2012. "An Investment Guide to Somaliland Opportunities & Conditions." Ministry of Commerce and Investment.

Wolfers, J. 2006. "Diagnosing Discrimination: Stock Returns and CEO Gender." *Journal of the European Economic Association* 4: 531–41.

World Bank. 2006. "Somalia: From Resilience Towards Recovery and Development." Country Economic Memorandum, World Bank, Washington, DC.

———. 2011. *Conflict, Security and Development, World Development Report 2011.* Washington, DC: World Bank.

———. 2012. "Private Sector Development and the Demand for Enterprise Support Grants in Somaliland: a Preliminary Look." David A. Phillips, Draft Report, World Bank, Washington, DC.

———. 2013. *Jobs, World Development Report 2013.* Washington, DC: World Bank.

———. 2013. "Migration and Development Brief 21." World Bank, Washington, DC.

———. 2014. *World Bank Global Financial Development Report.* Washington, DC: World Bank.

———. 2014. "GDP in Somaliland: A Preliminary Estimate for 2012." Unpublished note, World Bank, Washington, DC.

———. 2014 "Review of the Market for Remittances in Somaliland on the Basis of the CPSS-World Bank General Principles for International Remittance Services." April 2014.

World Bank and IFC. 2012. "Doing Business in Hargeisa, 2012." World Bank, Washington, DC.

Environmental Benefits Statement

The World Bank is committed to reducing its environmental footprint. In support of this commitment, the Publishing and Knowledge Division leverages electronic publishing options and print-on-demand technology, which is located in regional hubs worldwide. Together, these initiatives enable print runs to be lowered and shipping distances decreased, resulting in reduced paper consumption, chemical use, greenhouse gas emissions, and waste.

The Publishing and Knowledge Division follows the recommended standards for paper use set by the Green Press Initiative. Whenever possible, books are printed on 50 percent to 100 percent postconsumer recycled paper, and at least 50 percent of the fiber in our book paper is either unbleached or bleached using Totally Chlorine Free (TCF), Processed Chlorine Free (PCF), or Enhanced Elemental Chlorine Free (EECF) processes.

More information about the Bank's environmental philosophy can be found at http://crinfo.worldbank.org/wbcrinfo/node/4.

green
press
INITIATIVE

www.ingramcontent.com/pod-product-compliance
Lightning Source LLC
Chambersburg PA
CBHW081508200326
41518CB00015B/2426

* 9 7 8 1 4 6 4 8 0 4 9 1 5 *